Also by the Author

The Place of Precious Things

This Mystery and I

The Little Book of Awareness

The Quiet Place Within

Talks With Temerlen

Transforming Negative Emotions

The Heart of Awareness

author@pantheonprosebooks.com

THE SILENT SELF

Consciousness Realizing Itself
Beyond the Mind

PETER INGLE

THE SILENT SELF

Copyright © 2023 by Peter Ingle

All Rights Reserved
Produced in the United States of America

First edition 2023

No part of this publication may be reproduced, store, or transmitted, in any form, or by any means, electronic, mechanical, photocopying, recording, or otherwise, without permission in writing from the author.

Library of Congress Cataloging-in-Publication Data

Ingle, Peter M.
The Silent Self

ISBN: 978-1-7367425-4-9

cover design by Olivia Ingle
cover image by Mathias Reding

pantheonprosebooks.com

The Silent Self

I am but a mode of transit for original spirit.

old man Tcheng

The Silent Self

Foreword

The essence of self-transformation is the realization that your customary feeling of self is not your consciousness of *being*. This becomes clear through the recognition that 'you' as conscious awareness can perceive the feeling of self that projects *in your mind* as a sense of 'I', 'me', 'my' life, 'my' problems, and 'my' suffering.

This feeling includes the sense of 'my' desire to reach and achieve the experience of awakening or enlightenment, which in turn means that, as long as consciousness is entangled in the feeling of self, any *attempt* to awaken remains rooted in the psychological realm of 'I' where it inevitably projects itself as the identity of a seeker, or of a teacher who warrants special recognition and devotion.

What is the truth about consciousness and identity? And how is this truth to be found in the deepest dimensions of your being? These questions lie at the heart of each exchange in this book whose goal is to encourage and inspire the true transformation of consciousness itself.

The Silent Self

CONTENTS

The Silence of Being 1

The Illusion of 'I' 13

Investigating 'I' 43

'I' and Consciousness 65

Understanding Negative Emotions 91

Echoes of the Mind 119

The Hologram of 'Me' 157

Conscious Transformation 169

The Silent Self

The Silence of Being

The way up and the way down
are one and the same.

Heraclitus

WHAT IS commonly called the higher Self refers to pure consciousness or awareness which is silent. It is not silent in the sense of how an object or voice is silent. It *is* the silent dimension of the presence of conscious awareness. This presence comprises more than the absence of sound. It is *being*. But the mind cannot register what being is. It needs a conceptual reference, so it calls it silence.

Aren't we trying to use the mind to engage the presence of awareness?

The mind can align with awareness but it cannot engage awareness directly. What it can do is create an atmosphere that is conducive to the presence of awareness. It can do this by thinking in terms of awareness and by stepping out of the way to allow the consciousness of awareness to realize itself. Both of these 'efforts' by the mind promote an atmosphere of silence and stillness that echoes awareness and enables awareness to realize itself.

If I am being aware of my body and mind, is this self-realization?

It is really self-observation, meaning that you are aware *of* the body and mind. But this is how self-realization starts. Usually the mind becomes aware of the body and views it as 'my' body. Then there is a recognition in the mind of thoughts passing through it, but there is not a distinction between thoughts and the sense of 'I' observing them. There is not enough space between them yet. Awareness may go on, however, to become aware of seeing the body, the mind, and the sense of 'I, and from there recognize that it is beyond all of them. This recognition is the true beginning of self-realization.

How important is it to be aware of time and space?

It is strange that, as a rule, we don't question time, space, existence, or the fact that we can be aware of all these. It can help to be aware of time and space, but more important is to be aware that you are right here, right now, in this place. If you do this without forcing it—without identifying with trying to do it—the rest will start to come by itself. Keep noticing what is around you. This includes everything: the outside world, your body, and your inner world. As you notice all these, add to them the realization that you are noticing them.

You mean focusing in the moment?

Focusing on being present in this moment. It is *always* now in terms of time and space because we cannot be anywhere in time except in this moment, or anywhere in space other than where we are right here, right now. *This is* time and space. Always. The only thing that can expand beyond these parameters is the consciousness of awareness which is infinite in terms of both time and space. This is what eternity means: always here and now in *the same moment*.

But we are always living right here and now.

Yes, but we usually include our thoughts, feelings, and activities first, then add the presence of awareness to them. It should be the other way around. Conscious presence first. Everything else after that. Life follows awareness. Awareness does not follow life. But we are not usually conscious of this.

So we should be determined about chasing each moment?

Don't let the idea of the moment become a means to your fulfillment. Don't chase it or try to grasp it. You are not really after the moment. Awareness is after itself, looking for itself, and it always finds itself here and now. But this moment of here and now is not the fish you are trying to catch. It is simply the environment in which awareness catches itself.

I understand conceptually what the fourth way means that we are asleep, but it doesn't go much further. I still feel awake.

The reason it can be difficult to grasp is that the moment we talk about it we are a little more awake, although not in the deepest sense of being awake. What is important to understand is that technically speaking, 'we' are not asleep. What is asleep is consciousness or awareness. We as the person walk and talk and plan and accomplish things during the day. But it all happens by itself. The Self of awareness is not consciously aware while it all happens. Even when your mind focuses on things, awareness is not in focus behind the mind. But this awareness can be conscious of itself. That is what awakening means. It means awareness becoming conscious of itself. We as the body-mind person do not awaken. We remain pretty much the same except there is more light in our life. This light resides as the realization of *being here*, and the more this realization deepens, the more the light brightens and expands.

Does what the fourth way call a man number five remember himself or herself differently than a man number four?

Yes. As we walk and talk and do things, awareness is not consciously aware of being behind the scenes as this happens. Self-remembering is intended as a foray into this awareness. It begins as an exercise where you try to be aware of yourself, conscious of yourself, at the same time that you are doing other things. Men number 1-2-3 mean people in whom awareness is in a dim or vacant state. They are not interested in the business of awareness because they think they are already awake. Men number 4 mean people who have learned about awareness and who want to nurture awareness with the goal of being consciously aware more often. Men number 5 mean people in whom awareness is consciously knowing itself as the awareness of the mind and body, as well the awareness of the sense of 'I'. Men number 6 mean people in whom this awareness is more or less permanently conscious of itself. Men number 7 mean people in whom awareness has completely, permanently, irreversibly transcended the body, mind, and entire notion of the person and the life of the person.

Why is the future such a strong temptation?

The future is a mental projection of what the future *might* look like, and it is usually accompanied by desire or hope or anxiety or fear. By contrast, the pure being behind awareness is formless and has no urgency or need to anchor itself in something else at a later time or other place. On the one hand it takes courage to let *everything* about your life collapse into the present moment, into the now, and to stay here. On the other hand, the future is an illusion and you are just giving up an illusion. That illusion is what collapses and leaves only the present. The reality is that it is always only the present, but we camouflage this fact with the idea of a future because it fortifies our sense of identity.

Can you talk about identification, what it is, why it happens?

Identification is a force, a pressure. It is the psychological gravity behind the tendency for awareness to be unwittingly drawn to and into thoughts, sensations, feelings, objects, and the visible world at large, and to attach itself to *all* of them. The power of conscious *being* is that it can override, resist, and neutralize this pull, and the miracle of the human form is that we can be a vehicle for pure being to actualize this possibility by realizing itself within us. We could stop here and explore what I just said for a long time because this is the whole thing, really. We are talking about the transformation and transmutation of divine matter consciously realizing itself *through* the conduit of a human being created for this purpose. This human form is a profound hinge in creation. We are a gateway that gives awareness the possibility of being transformed as it passes through this gateway of human existence.

Can you say more about the silence of awareness being different than what we usually think of as silence?

It means that awareness does not manifest through a form that our body, intellect, and emotions can relate to, so they interpret *its effect on them* as silence and emptiness. The pure being of awareness, however, does not experience itself as silence and emptiness. It knows itself as the fullness of being comprising silence and emptiness.

Why can't the mind understand this as we talk about it right now?

Because the mind—the intellectual center—can understand only concepts. It cannot step out of itself and out of concepts. Only awareness can do that. As clever as the intellect seems to be, it always comes up against the wall of a concept *about* awareness. You can see this right now. We as the mind are talking about awareness. Our awareness of this is not the discussion, the words, the idea. It is the real thing.

But the mind is being affected and knows it is being affected. It knows it is being made more aware.

The house—meaning the mind and body—does not actually become aware of itself, but it can comprehend that it is being filled with light—with awareness—although it does not fully know what this means because what it experiences is limited to thought and sensation. When the house warms up as the sun shines in it, the house registers in its own way the reflection of light and heat, but the house does not register light itself or the source of light. Even the ability of the mind and body to register things comes from awareness itself. It is perceiving *through* them. The body and mind themselves do not perceive.

What is the relationship between what the fourth way calls essence and higher centers?

We can say that essence aware of itself transforms as the higher emotional center, and that the higher emotional center aware of itself transforms as the higher intellectual center. This is a fourth way description of how the consciousness of awareness expands out if itself as more and more consciousness of being aware. But this description is provided as a way for the mind to think about it. In actuality it refers to the contractions and expansions of consciousness itself. For instance, the ego is an extreme contraction of consciousness into a form where it is no longer aware of itself as consciousness. Essence is a much less contracted form of simple awareness out of which the consciousness of awareness can expand, and expand again, and again.

How do you define perception?

Perception means seeing. But there is a difference between seeing with the mind and body, and seeing with awareness *as awareness.* Also, the clearer and deeper the perception, the less it can be reflected in the human mind. You find this in painting and music where perceptions are conveyed without words or thoughts which are too dense to capture certain perceptions. There are also perceptions that painting and music cannot contain because they belong solely to the dimension of pure consciousness. The highest truth cannot be spoken or conveyed in human form.

Who is aware of being aware?

That depends. Not being aware is one thing. Being aware is another thing. Being aware of being aware is another. And being aware as the pure being behind awareness is yet another. What we call Brahman or god or the absolute refers to the farthest, deepest dimension of pure being which is beyond the sense of being a person who is aware. Another way to answer your question is that personality—the ego—can be aware. Or essence can be aware. Or awareness can be aware. Or awareness can be conscious of its own awareness. It depends on where your being is in your galaxy in a given moment.

Why is the feeling of 'I' so hard to shake off?

Because we are so accustomed to believing it and wanting to believe it. What thinks 'I', feels like 'I', says 'I', and reacts as 'I' stems from the psychological notion of being a person in this body and mind. It is a projection in the mind, very much like a hologram, and consciousness is identified with it. Identification also fuels our *belief* in the hologram, which keeps the projection alive. We are convinced that it is who we are, yet there is much more to us than this. Consciousness is not the body or the mind or the feeling of 'I' in relation to the body and mind. It is aware of all of them and upon realizing this it recognizes itself. At that point there is nothing to shake off.

Why do I feel afraid as awareness grows?

The fear is likely a result of the ego having its psychological perch of identity disturbed. This disturbance is felt in the instinctive center and the emotional center which creates confusion in the intellectual center. Notice, too, your question: "Why am 'I' afraid?" Who is this 'I'? That is the thing to notice. Realize also that awareness is seeing this 'I' and the reaction surrounding it. Don't be afraid of the fear. Try to move toward awareness instead. This is important to understand because there is a strong temptation to analyze, sort out, and try to resolve our fears. As a result, awareness gets identified all over again.

To me the fourth way system feels like a closed fist: tight and rigid.

A system like the fourth way is, at first, for the mind. It is designed to orient the mind in favor of consciousness. It seems tight because it is tight to the mind as well as to the emotions. But the system is also multi-layered. There are depths in certain ideas which only conscious awareness can plumb. These depths in the system which the mind cannot grasp are meant to serve consciousness itself. Not all ideas have the same density and vibration. In the beginning the system may seem like a thick, heavy blueprint. But the deeper you go into it, the lighter and more transparent it becomes.

Is the pain body associated with emotional repression?

The pain body, as Eckhart Tolle calls it, can be seen as a conglomeration of 'I's that have habituated themselves to a negative point of view about the past or future in a way that keeps your underlying sense of 'me' behind them intact. The pain body is your physiological body and your psychological body cooperating to bury *and preserve* painful feelings of 'I'. Upon knowing this, or at least knowing about this concept, many people concentrate on the buried part but not always on the preserving part. Something wants to hold onto the feeling of 'I' in the pain body. What if that something could let go of the feeling of 'I' being preserved? And what if you as consciousness could let go of both?

What do you think would happen?

It is a question for you to explore in yourself. I could say something but it ultimately has to come from your own investigation without words.

Can you say anything more about the pain body itself?

The instinctive center serves as the central circuit of the four centers. It regulates the *physical* energy of the other centers. Chief feature then pumps impulses into this circuit where they take the form of *psychological* urges that drive the centers. The feeling of 'I' assembles around this apparatus and, as a result of their influence, it can turn negative at a moment's notice. As this happens over and over again, it digs grooves in the psyche and we resort to settling into these grooves when circumstances aren't to our liking. These grooves are created by pain and they *give us* pain when we resort to them. It is a deeply entrenched pattern that we repeat because we like it. The question is, why do we like clinging to these grooves of identity?

Because it draws more attention to ourselves?

This is true in the sense that it draws more attention to the deeply felt sense of self. Another way to see it is that the physical body exists on the earth and will go back into the earth, whereas the pain body is for the moon. In fourth way parlance, it sends negatively charged energy to the moon which feeds the magnetic field of the moon. Neither the physical body nor the pain body form by accident. They exist for specific purposes within the larger mechanism of the solar system. But the pain body is not necessary, just as the ego is not necessary. They are only necessary for staying asleep.

So the pain body wants to suffer?

It is not that the pain body *wants* to suffer. It is that we attach a sense of identity to the suffering. Sometimes the suffering is real but often it is imagined, meaning it is just a reflection of our imaginary picture of ourselves. In either case, the pain body does not exist as a separate entity, just as the ego does not exist as a separate entity. Without identification, neither can form as an identity. So the idea behind the pain body is to see how the negative side of our psychology accrues the habit of imagining an identity around suffering. The fourth way calls this 'unnecessary suffering' because we don't need it and can survive without it, just as we can survive without the ego once we realize what this means.

~ ~ ~

The Illusion of 'I'

Destroy the ego by seeking its identity. It will automatically vanish and reality will shine forth by itself. This is the direct method.

Ramana Maharshi

THE NOTION of yourself as 'I' and 'me' does not exist as an actual entity. It exists as a mental image that is projected through the body as behavior. It takes form as a psychological entity that in turn drives physical action. When these manifestations are infused with the force of negativity they solidify even further and can become petrified. You see this in some older people whose notion of themselves as 'I' has etched itself permanently into their facial expression, posture, and demeanor. The more identified you are, the deeper your sense of 'I' gets entrenched in form. Conversely, the less identified you are, the more simple your sense of 'I' becomes—all the way to the point where it *un*forms and dissolves back into its original substance as essence and pure consciousness.

Why is it so easy for us to become negative?

Because the *possibility* of becoming negative is always waiting, even when we are feeling good. One slight tun and we become negative. Most human beings live in a state of mechanical readiness where they are *always* poised to transfer and discharge negative energy. This is the physiological and psychological basis on which humanity operates and is supposed to operate. It is no accident that so many people become negative so often. Identification and negativity comprise a sort of electric current that vivifies humanity, but the energy behind the current comes originally from consciousness.

What do you mean by mechanical readiness?

Identification. Envision yourself not identified. Completely not identified and fully present rather than always on the verge of being identified and becoming negative in response to things.

Has a man number five escaped from the body?

What the fourth way calls a man number five refers to consciousness having transcended the identity of 'I' in the mind and body. Consciousness is free *inside* the mind and body but it is still inside so to speak. The next step is when it starts to realize itself independently of the mind and body and your whole person, which represents the idea of a man number six.

How can I be sure of that?

Only by experiencing it for yourself—as conscious awareness. You should not believe what I just said, but you may want to think about it and try to connect it to your understanding of what self-remembering means.

Is creation an illusion the same way 'I' is an illusion?

Illusion does not mean that something does not exist. It means it is being perceived in a false or distorted or incomplete way, usually through the faculties of the mind. What we call creation is highly complex, extraordinary, and mesmerizing, so it is easy for awareness to forget itself and identify with all the *forms* of creation. It is easy for it to remain simply aware *of* things. From there it is a big step for it to realize that it is *aware of seeing* creation, and later to realize that it is *both the seeing and the being aware of seeing*. And even later that it is everything: the seen, the seeing, the awareness of seeing, and the being behind seeing. As Lao Tzu said, "From this mysterious well flows all existence."

Is it helpful to pray for abundance?

Most people think of abundance as plenitude in the sense of overflowing. But it can also be seen as a-bound-ance, meaning without a boundary, which is a characteristic of consciousness. But abundance does not mean that your life will be more full and wonderful and wealthy. It means your true being is limitless. So when you pray for abundance, think in terms of consciousness expanding into the infinity of itself.

Can you say more about why thoughts are not necessary?

They are not necessary in terms of knowing who and what we really are, which is the consciousness of awareness. Thoughts stem from this consciousness, but they are not consciousness. They are reflections of consciousness in the mirror of the mind. This is not easy to comprehend because we operate almost entirely from thought, not from direct perception. Which means we are living our lives according to reflections, not perceptions of reality. As we are driven by thoughts in the mind, consciousness looms as the background from which thoughts arise, yet it is unaware of itself as the background because it has established itself as a sense of identity in the mind. It is within this experience of identity that we try to resolve our sense of identity, the meaning of our life, and the solution to our suffering. But none of these things can ever be resolved by thoughts in the mind.

My problem with thoughts is the tension they cause both in my mind and in my body.

Although we experience tense thoughts, the cause of the tension is not so much in thoughts themselves. It is in the structure of the mind. Can you see the difference? The furniture in the room does not become tense by itself. The walls and floor and ceiling tighten and this tightening gives rise to tension in their contents. Conversely, if we can remove tension from the structure, that immediately affects the contents. This is what meditation and yoga really mean, or should mean: neutralizing and minimizing tension in the *structure* of the mind and the body. The idea is to loosen the energy that is pent up in the four centers and release it to consciousness. The purpose of self-remembering is to harness this energy consciously.

Isn't that also the goal of therapy and medication?

Therapy tries to resolve conflicts within the contents of the mind and body by making adjustments to the ego and the ego's idea of its relationship to the body. Medicine, on the other hand, directs chemical influences to the structure of the centers—mainly the instinctive center—with the goal of neutralizing the instinctive center's influence over the other centers. But scientists and doctors do not understand it in this exact way. They don't know about the different centers and they don't recognize the distinction between the four centers, the ego, and awareness.

Are there better ways to heal awareness?

From one point of view, awareness is complete and does not need fixing. At the same time, essence is your purest nature and this effervescence is what transforms as conscious awareness. So it is the seedcase for awareness. Healing almost always refers to your ego and its inflations as a personality, but sometimes healing involves essence, too, especially if it has been traumatized. But for the most part, healing means reestablishing the proper connection and balance of personality in relation to essence. Even an essence that has suffered terribly—and sometimes because of it—retains its resiliency as the foundation for transformation.

Why do there seem to be so many people posturing a spiritual identity?

Some people start and finish their search for enlightenment in the ego because they latch onto an *idea* of enlightenment and then project that *image* as themselves. They convince themselves and want to convince other people that they are spiritually advanced. The other reason is that enlightenment has its roots in essence. Essence is your true nature in the sense that it is a simple state of *being*. The feeling of identity as 'I' forms later in the shell of personality that accumulates around essence. But essence does not experience itself as an identity. It experiences itself as simply *being* here, which is what you see in the eyes of infants. Sometimes spiritual seekers rightly discover simply *being* at their core, but instead of awareness realizing itself inherent in essence—like a beam of light running through a delicate thread—the feeling of being gets appropriated by the ego in the form of a spiritual personality. In other words, the seeker steps onto the threshold of pure being only to get lured back into the familiarity and comfort of 'I'.

I often experience so much torment and confusion that I feel helpless. Then later I find myself out if it but I don't know how. And then again I am back in it.

Everything that happens in the mind and body does not happen to consciousness. Consciousness simply sees it happening. So even though the feeling of 'I' is being shaped and shifted and tormented by energy in the different centers, consciousness itself remains free. All it has to do is realize this. It is a small step that seems huge from the perspective of 'I'. But from the perspective of conscious awareness it is tiny. It is just a matter of *being conscious of being here* while the machinations of the mind play themselves out. In this way, awareness extracts itself from the substance of the energy in the four centers.

When an internal storm comes, find your way as best you can to the center of it where things are calm. Or see if you can make your way to a place outside the storm, beyond the geography of the storm. Both of these places—deep inside and all the way outside—are tied to each other. And the key to reaching them is non-identification. That means not fighting the storm and not allowing it to suck you into its whirlwind. Next time a storm passes and you find yourself safely out if it, take a deep drink of that feeling and remember it so you can recall it the next time the storm sweeps through you.

Can awareness heal the body?

When consciousness is acutely aware, you can feel a healing energy passing from consciousness to the centers. They start to normalize and their contents start to quiet down and even dissolve. This is very different than working directly with the contents of centers; for example by trying to unravel the story of 'me' or revisit the trauma of 'I'. The reason it is different is because when consciousness is not identified it *enables* a transference of energy from itself to the centers without any reference to the ego or any attempts to heal the ego. Consciousness simply brings the centers back into alignment and this realignment allows healing to happen by itself. This will not heal a broken bone or an infection, but it will neutralize the body in such a way that the body can better heal itself.

How is attention distinct from consciousness, or is it?

Attention is a manifestation of consciousness *through* the four centers. Each center has its own form of attention, but behind all of them and passing through them is the same 'substance' of consciousness. You can also think of consciousness sending a portion of itself on an errand as attention. It is also useful to envision consciousness without any association to the four centers; without a mind and body. What we think of as attention would be very different. It would not exist in the same way because consciousness would not need to manifest *through* anything.

Is the mind basically an interior universe?

In many ways, yes. When you look at it closely you see that the inner world reflects the outer world. Our personality, essence, and consciousness mirror different dimensions of the universe. According to the fourth way, this is because they stem from the same energy inherent in those dimensions and they are manifestations of that same energy in human form.

Gurdjieff mentioned but did not elaborate on the sex center as a fifth lower center. Can you comment?

Very little is known or can be detected about the sex center as a fifth center because its energy is so incredibly fast and volatile. The fourth way theory is that it is behind the formation and procreative impulses of all the other centers combined. It is like the furnace that provides energy for the instinctive center which in turn fuels the other centers, so its operations are even less discernible than those of the instinctive center. At the same time, the energy of the sex center derives from the same pure being as conscious awareness and we can sometimes intuit this in our sexual relations with other humans.

Such intuition, however, is easily distorted and perverted, first by the instinctive center, and then by the other centers in a sort of cascading effect of the misappropriation of this very fine, very delicate, very pure energy. Another reason the sex center is hard to discern and capture is because in its purest condition it is urgently readying its rarefied energy to explode into a proliferation of form—which can also be detected in violent expressions of negativity. In the simplest sense, we lose this energy forever when we express negative emotions.

What is the connection between sex energy and sex?

Pure sex energy and pure sex are mystical phenomena. But you have to be careful not to take this the wrong way on the physical level. In their highest form, sex and sex energy are not physical or molecular. They are metaphysical and electronic. The pure energy of the sex center is the basic energy of life. For the most part, what we can detect about the sex center is how its energy manifests through the instinctive center; for instance, when the instinctive center evaluates another instinctive center as a potential target or mate. This happens at lightning speed as a mechanism of procreation, but the instinctive center experiences it as lust and desire, and fantasy often enters in. Pure sex is devoid of all three of these. It might best be described as the ecstasy of union, but even this is easily misinterpreted. Conscious union is very different from physical union.

What about sex energy apart from sex itself?

There is a vitality behind each person's identity. It is a certain degree of magnetism. It manifests through the instinctive center but has its origin in the sex center. Sometimes it is pure. Sometimes it is heavy. Sometimes it is distorted, or has become distorted, in some way. It has a chemical basis but it cannot be scientifically measured, and it is elusive to perception. It is also very explosive, like gunpowder or flammable fuel. And it can contribute to explosions of negativity, especially violent explosions, as well as perversion and abuse. This energy is the core material of life, and it can destroy as well as create.

Because it is so explosive, does that mean it is out of our control?

You cannot control sex energy directly. If you think you can it is the instinctive center thinking so and trying to. What you *can* control is identification. It is like controlling the reins on the horse. You cannot control the horse itself but you can steer it by harnessing identification. This analogy makes it sound easy, which it is not. Best not to tamper with the sex center. The right solution is to be present, not identify, not express negative emotions, and learn to transform the energy behind negative emotions by exposing the ego. The cause of the wrong work of the sex center and the distortions of its energy are due to malformations in the ego. When sex energy gets appropriated as a sense of the ego, that is where the problems begin. That is when purity starts to become impure.

We are in the universe right now. Don't you find that amazing?

The more aware consciousness is, the more it marvels at what we call the universe. Behind what we see is a vast phenomena that boggles the mind. And consciousness is even more vast. It is no small thing that consciousness can perceive the universe and be aware of doing so.

Do you think the solar system is conscious of itself?

The solar system has a body and may also have a mind and essence and even consciousness that we are not cognizant of. The same may be true of the galaxy. We don't know. If those dimensions and cosmoses do contain some aspect of consciousness, it would seem to also be restricted to those forms until they decay and die. But maybe not.

Doesn't the fourth way view the universe as a body or as having a body?

According to the fourth way, the ray of creation—what we call the universe—is akin to a body with three stories: an instinctive-moving center, an emotional center, and an intellectual center, with the earth and moon comprising the lower story. In this arrangement, organic life on earth is akin to the stomach of the solar system. Lots going on here. Lots of absorption and digestion and conversion of matter into different forms of energy. The idea is that humanity is a cog in the wheel of the solar system which in turn is a cog in the galaxy. Nothing exists by itself or for only itself.

How does essence fit into that wheel?

The idea of essence is that it is a seedcase of pure consciousness, a drop of which is planted in this seed so that it might bloom out of this seed. This is also designed into the arrangement of humanity as part of organic life on earth within the solar system and galaxy. Think of it like this: the absolute pure being at the source of consciousness extends itself as the manifestation of all forms throughout its entire body of the universe, but the consciousness inherent in these forms is not conscious of itself. One exception, and possibly the only exception, is essence within a human being which is a simple form of *being* that can, but does not always, realize its beingness—which we experience as the sense of being here in this place at this moment on earth. From this simple realization, consciousness can expand its realization of being aware all the way back to its absolute origin.

And the moon is responsible for identification?

It is not responsible. It is a third force—an outside influence—that enables identification to unfold in human beings. The physical and psychological 'pull' that we experience as identification is due in large part to the pressure of the moon bearing down on the earth. This pressure is also under the influence of direct as well as reflected sunlight. So the sun is equally if not more involved. Together, the sun and moon are pushing and pulling influences *through* the earth and *to* the moon to nourish the moon. All of this is connected in ways that we cannot see, and we are caught in the middle imagining that we control our lives. It is no accident that our moon is so large compared to the earth and so close in its orbit around the earth. Both factors contribute to the force of its pull on us.

But it is just a theory...

Everything is theory until it becomes reality for you. In the case of the moon and identification, you can dismiss it or you can borrow it as a lens for thinking in a new way, in a bigger way than we are accustomed to thinking. From one point of view, the entire fourth way system is just that: an assortment of lenses to help the intellect broaden, deepen, and expand its view in such a way that we are less identified, and so that the seed of *being* in our essence can start to open and bloom. Most people never think deeply about the fact that they are a human being on a planet in a solar system in a vast galaxy. And even fewer people *realize* it because their essence is encrusted inside a strong personality and entrenched in the concerns of the ego.

But a less identified mind is still the mind, isn't it? Just with a different point of view?

Your question is coming from the mind thinking about non-identification. Yes, non-identification has an effect on the mind, but ultimately it is not about the mind because the mind is not what becomes identified in the first place. Consciousness is what gets identified and being less identified is about consciousness becoming conscious of itself. The mind can *think* about being in the universe whereas consciousness *realizes* itself in the midst of the universe. The more consciousness retracts itself from the pull of identification, the more profoundly you realize your existence on earth, in the solar system, and within the universe. The mystery of creation starts to reveal hints about itself.

Is it true to say that the more identified we are the harder it is to remember ourselves?

It feels like that at first, but in actuality, consciousness can come back into full focus *immediately* at any time in any circumstance, whether it be enmeshed in a strong emotion or lost in an activity at work. Sometimes, the more difficult the circumstances, the better the result of coming back into focus can be because it makes the contrast between consciousness and what it has been identified with strikingly obvious. If this realization is strong enough, it becomes possible for consciousness to start focusing its awareness of itself at any time.

What this means is that even when you find yourself immersed in an extreme thought, or a dark mood, or the tumultuous memory of a volatile and painful situation, consciousness can pull out of those and out of the notion of identity it had invested in them, and *be itself* as pure consciousness. It is like a beach full of sand that is overtrodden with footprints, or a body of water that is in turmoil, being suddenly swept smooth again and calmed because the energy that had been disturbing them has funneled back to its source. The form of the sand and the shape of the water are no longer enlivened by the energy of consciousness, so they collapse. They disappear. Even if they try to reappear later, conscious awareness 'knows' not to invest itself in them.

I understand what you said earlier about the question coming from my mind, and that is what I am wrestling with. I can't seem to go from thinking about being less identified to actually being less identified.

The air in a room does not cling to any objects in the room. It just surrounds them. This is what the awareness of our consciousness should do, but instead it clings. It is pressured to cling, but it does not have to succumb to this pressure. To understand this, you have to look into your being, see what all this means for yourself, and understand how it could be different. Throw away all the terminology such as consciousness and awareness and identification and ego. Look directly at your experience of existence and *being*. Why are you not more conscious of being here, not only as a person, but as consciousness itself? Why is this consciousness not recognizing and retaining awareness of itself? Everything else we talk about is connected to this.

How does non-identification apply to what you call the structure of centers as opposed to their content?

We usually notice, to some extent, the activity going on within each center of the mind and body, meaning the thoughts, emotions, sensations, and movements that comprise the contents of the centers. We have to be more aware to notice their structures and the vibration of their structures. When we are identified, the structures of centers are vibrating which in turn agitates their contents. It may be an intense or slight vibration, depending on the degree of identification. Rarely are the structures completely free of all vibration. When they are, there is great relaxation and conservation of energy. All momentum ceases and you are firmly established in the present. And it is not because you neutralized all the contents—all the 'I's—*in* the centers. It is because their structures are no longer reverberating with identification. Instead they are aligning with pure consciousness.

So just noticing the structure calms down the vibration?

Yes. As you become familiar with recognizing the vibration, you can neutralize identification at that point rather than trying to calm down your thoughts or emotions or movements. Instead of struggling directly against swirling thoughts, tumultuous emotions, and harried movements, you go directly to their structure, notice it, sense its vibration, and become consciously aware of sensing it. Just noticing the mind or body starts to change their chemistry and operation, which in turn affects whatever activity is going on inside them. This is something that is at the heart of the fourth way system, although it gets overlooked: that transformation is brought about by the combination of *conscious* self-observation and self-remembering, which are aspects of the same thing.

How to better see the structure? What are we looking for?

The body gives rise to sensations and movement. The mind gives rise to thought and emotion. In fourth way language, this means sensations in the instinctive center, movements in the moving center, thoughts in the intellectual center, and emotions in the emotional center. With sustained observation you can notice the difference between all four. You can 'taste' how each is distinct. As you do, you can realize that there is something behind them, holding them, projecting them. Thoughts spring out of and into the mind, almost like fireworks in the sky. Sensations do the same within the boundary of the body. So, instead of concentrating on *what* is being projected, you try to notice *where* it is being projected from. You just notice it.

And then?

It is like being in a room full of noisy people. Instead of trying to calm each of them down, you move to the back of the room where the door is and just lean against the wall. In doing so you don't change any of the people; you change your position in relation to all of them. You let go your identification with them. Then you realize you can slip out the door if you want to. The people remain, and the room they are in remains, but you transform.

Why is the ego such a barrier in spiritual work?

It is useful to consider how your intellect and emotions would function if there was no ego. There would be no central psychological point of reference to establish a sense of identity around, and no sense of identity to experience itself *in relation to* the world. Your perceptions would no longer have anything to do with 'you'. They would be only about the nature of perception itself.

This is exactly the case with essence in small children. Essence is very close to realizing itself as conscious awareness, but it is *unaware* of this capacity in itself. As a result it gets immersed in fascination with *what* it sees. Over time, the simple *being* of essence becomes coated with and covered over by the conditioning of life which causes it to develop a sense of identity that becomes the focal point of our life. Along the way the simple consciousness of being gets more or less completely obscured. So it is not really that the ego is a barrier. It is that essence unwittingly *becomes* a sense of ego.

Can we actually counteract the pull of the moon?

Neutralize might be a better word. The force of the moon exerts a magnetic pull on all of organic life around the surface of the earth. In the case of the four centers of our body and mind, it pulls especially on the lower, more dense parts of our being. It drums up memories, nostalgia, regrets, hopes, fears, guilt, dark thoughts, notions of revenge, and more. And because awareness is usually identified with the mind and body, it gets pulled into this running stream of sensations, thoughts, and emotions. But it is due to identification. Consciousness itself is not subject to the influence of the moon. Only when it collapses into identification does it become prey for the magnet of the moon. Think of the consciousness in billions of people on earth being sucked into this magnetic field. Then envision a group of people in whom this is not happening.

Can you draw a distinction between pure being and awareness and attention?

From an absolute source that I call pure being there is an emanation of itself in the form of consciousness or awareness. Emanating from them is what we know as attention. And then, as we get identified, attention becomes even less conscious and gets more and more immersed in whatever it is aware *of* and engaged with. Envision a miniscule thread of undetectable pure being surrounded by a slightly thicker, still invisible, but now detectable thread of light, which is in turn surrounded by an even thicker cord of material called attention, which in turn gets coated in a very coarse and thick material called identification. All of these are different degrees of consciousness from thin to thick, from fine to coarse, from transparent to opaque, from fast to slow. It is all different dimensions of consciousness.

What is the source of identification? I don't mean the influence of the moon. I mean what does the moon actually influence?

Try to envision being *completely* absent of identification. No identity. Completely untouched by thoughts and emotions and sensations, and not attached to any outward perceptions. Just pure consciousness nestled in a condition of being itself aware of itself. This is the source of pure being which is also the starting point of identification. From this point, consciousness somehow is drawn to go looking for itself in the many forms of its own manifestations which include the entire universe and, in our case, the psychological and physical realms of the human body.

Pure being is sort of like the top of your head and the moon is sort of like your toe all the way at the other end of creation. The toe says, "Come look at me, be me, and worry about me." And consciousness gets pulled into the toe. As humans on earth we reside let's say in the ankle. Inside us there is a special seed of consciousness that can sprout in such a way that it starts to realize it is not the toe, and this realization can extend all the way back up to the head; back to the source of itself that it came from. This self-returning is what self-remembering is about.

You mentioned a moment ago that essence becomes a sense of identity that we experience as the ego. Is that correct?

Yes. All these aspects of ourselves—essence, personality, attention, awareness—are initially explained as separate things because the mind cannot see them as manifestations and representations of the same thing in different form. It has to be given this information in separate pieces. A more complete picture is that the ego is a form that consciousness takes on as a result of identification. But this formation is also perceptible to the consciousness it springs from. That is how we can see and know the ego. As the ego, consciousness longs for a sense of fulfillment that it imagines it will find somewhere else at some other time in some other way. It is not content because it is always looking in the wrong direction for contentment. It is existing *in relation to* an idea of the past and the future and even the present rather than relating to itself *as* consciousness. It may sound preposterous, but the ego is actually an imaginary identity imagining an imaginary idea of itself in a past, in a present, and in a future. It is a dream of identity in form which formless consciousness is projecting within itself.

But doesn't consciousness long for the present?

There is no longing in consciousness. Longing is an activity of the mind. Consciousness is simply here now. It is just obscured by the mental gyrations of past and future, and by the imaginary pressure these gyrations impose on the ego, one of which is a sense of longing. It is also true that consciousness implants in the mind a desire for presence so that this urge in the mind will point consciousness back to itself as consciousness.

Does 'I' know when it disappears?

'I' does not recognize its disappearance just as it does not recognize its appearance. Why? Because 'I' does not exist. It is a mental phantom. You as consciousness are always there behind the notion of 'I' experiencing yourself through 'I', but you don't know it. You don't know yourself as pure consciousness. The consciousness in you is not aware of itself. This is the basis of enlightenment, awakening, spirituality. If you understand this, you are starting to step out of the illusion.

If everything is one thing, why do they seem like so many different things?

All sand art is the same sand in different forms. The forms are illusory as objects. They are just sand. But we don't see the sand. We see the objects. The physical world is the same. And our psychological world is also the same. They are all based on the raw material of consciousness manifesting in different dimensions in different forms. But the mind can only interpret them one at a time, separately.

Can you give an example?

You can notice right now that words are symbols for sounds. They even include silent sounds, such as the spaces between letters, syllables, and words. The mind learns to interpret these sounds into meaning—both the literal meaning of definitions and the nuanced meaning that comes from voice inflections, emphasis, cadence, and so on. It is astonishing how sounds, language, letters, words, and meaning are really connected as one thing in different forms, but we hardly notice this fact.

Is the same thing true about how we decide something and then do it?

In a sense, yes. But what you describe is not a conscious activity. What most people experience as decision-making and doing are the result of a partnership between chief feature and the instinctive center. These two influences are behind most of our actions, but we don't notice them. They just happen and we experience a combined feeling of 'I' am deciding and 'I' am doing this. This is how humanity operates most of the time. Rarely is anyone acting from the awareness of pure consciousness.

How do you see the difference between the progressive way and the direct path?

There are several ways of understanding the differences. But before that it helps to understand the similarity. Both approaches point to and lead to the same consciousness of awareness beyond the mind. This is the main thing to remember. That said, you can think of the progressive way as a pushing from below and the direct path as a pulling from above.

For example, the progressive way comprises a series of methods for working from the bottom-up; from unawareness to awareness; from what awareness is not to what awareness is; from the mind learning and trying to understand that there is something beyond the mind; and in this way enabling consciousness to realize itself outside the mind. The direct path, on the other hand, is a top-down approach with only one method which is to pursue the reality that you are consciousness; not to think about it or try to do something to achieve it; but to focus on being it since you already are that.

The fact is, however, that the direct path is not so direct for many people because it requires a subtle nuance of perception that is elusive to sustain in the face of myriad thoughts, emotions, sensations, and feelings of 'I' that are constantly presenting themselves to consciousness. On the other side, the progressive way can be equally distracting because it is easy to get caught up in ideas and practices and lose sight of consciousness itself.

Why do you think anxiety is on the rise in the modern world?

Anxiety is the result of conflict in the ego. It can stem from the instinctive center or the emotional center or both, but the effect is felt in a person's sense of security as an identity. It is hard to pinpoint the exact cause of this rise, but it seems safe to say that it is connected to a parallel rise in electronic communication, negative news, and cultural upheavals around the world, and the effect these are having on our sense of identity, safety, and well being. It is also clear that the increases in technology, thought to improve our lives, have brought increasing isolation. And the isolation is physical as well as psychological.

For instance, large box stores and online shopping have replaced the emotional connection to your local grocer, banker, doctor. Neighbors don't know each other or spend time together. Family structures and extended family networks are weakening. At the same time there is an upsurge in migration and integration. Something new is happening to the fabric of humanity and to the chemistry of organic life on earth, and anxiety is one result of these changes.

How can we develop unconditional love?

Unconditional love is not about me or you as persons loving things unconditionally. There is just love as a kind of perfume that is a natural byproduct of conscious awareness. It happens as a result of perceiving unconditionally without expectations, demands, and requirements that anything be other than it is. The less you are identified, the greater the chance of love manifesting in its place.

Isn't acceptance a way toward love?

Acceptance can be a way of lessening your identification with expectations, demands, and requirements. But there is a difference between making an effort to be more accepting and actually perceiving with full openness. One is in the mind. The other is beyond the mind. The effort in the mind can easily give way to identification again and be displaced by judgment. So you need to be on guard against trying to love for its own sake, or for wanting to be a better person in your eyes and the eyes of others, which is ego-based.

I feel like I am often the victim of circumstances that are making me suffer, so I blame the circumstances and feel sorry for myself. I can't get out of this pattern.

What is happening is just happening. It is not happening on purpose to 'you'. Try to take the idea of yourself as a unique identity out of the equation and look at the bigger picture. Plants and animals don't take things personally. The only reason we do is because we have an ego that gets projected between perception and reality. You can also use the times when you are in this pattern to look more carefully at the feeling of 'I' who feels like circumstances and other people are conspiring to make you suffer. How do you experience the suffering and victim-hood? Precisely what does it feel like? What negative emotions accompany it and defend it? Do you fight back with anger or want to fight back but are afraid to? Do you get angry inside and roil in resentment? What sensations surround the self-pity that engulfs you? Who do you complain to? Who do you blame? There is a lot of material here for scrutinizing the ego, not with judgment but with clear observation.

If you can shine the light of awareness all the way into this cavern of identity and be honest with yourself about what you see, you will take a tremendous step and free a lot of energy. It will also take more than one trip into the cavern, so be patient. Realize, too, that you are not the only person who feels this way and gets trapped in this cycle. Part of what keeps us trapped is that we think we are unique, that our problems are unique, that our inability to resolve them is unique, and that we are uniquely inadequate because of all of these. It is a perfect atmosphere for fueling the ego.

~ ~ ~

Investigating 'I'

I am alpha and omega,
the beginning and the end.

John the Evangelist

THE INQUIRY 'who am I' can also be turned around and investigated as 'I am who'. The first is meant to prompt consciousness and lead you out of the mind. The second is meant to highlight how consciousness, as it identifies, *becomes* the ego. Both are also incomplete because consciousness is not an 'I'. It is beyond 'I'. It encompasses 'I'. This is true even when, as a result of identification, consciousness gets appropriated as a sense of 'I'.

When you were suggesting to a lady how to scrutinize the ego during periods of victim-hood, I thought of chief feature and that it might be playing a part in all that? Would you agree?

Chief feature is almost always behind our most frequent and most intense negative emotions. As is the case with many people, the feature of vanity plays a large part. But there is more to it than that because each chief feature thinks it is unique, which is an aspect of vanity. In the same way, each chief feature is also compensation for a feeling of fear that is peculiar to each feature. How a person approaches the idea of minimizing their chief feature is often a reflection of their chief feature.

For example, 'dominance' thinks that chief feature can be regulated and even be useful when properly controlled, and it is no accident that people with dominance are highly prone to regulating and controlling themselves, other people, and circumstances. 'Tramp' on the other hand doesn't take the idea of chief feature seriously. It shrugs off the idea even though it likes to ridicule others for their chief features. And, again, it is no accident that people with tramp are prone to not valuing themselves or what might be good for them, so they end up shirking responsibility with the attitude that things aren't that important and don't really matter. 'Vanity' is either worried that other people will see its chief feature and judge it for being vain, in which case it avoids situations where it might fail; or it inflates its image of itself and tries constantly to get attention to keep its image inflated. 'Non-existence' is not sure how to proceed in relation to chief feature and does not actively pursue it, which is true about most of a person's life who has a chief feature of non-existence.

Chief feature is a worthwhile study, and can be a very practical tool for self-observation. It is about much more than external behavior. It is about the psychological roots that drive behavior.

How is chief feature also connected to the instinctive center?

It is connected in the sense that it is part of our physiological makeup when we are born. The fourth way explains this in a more complete way with the idea of body types, and how each type is prone to a specific chief feature as well as a set of complementary features. Chief feature begins as a tendency inherent in essence. It is only when we develop a personality around essence that chief feature becomes a governing characteristic of our personality. This happens as the tendency manifests through our psychology as well as our physiology. For instance, chief feature enters into most of our emotional decisions and accounts for how we react to other people and situations. The other big area is how features are prone to different kinds of negative emotions. All of these things tie together and inform the identity we experience as 'I'.

So 'I' is the veil that keeps us asleep?

Yes. This veil is also a trap in the sense that the awareness of consciousness is trapped in it but can slip out of it by seeing 'I' as just a psychological image—a projection in the mind—and realizing itself as the consciousness which is aware of 'I'. Another way to say it is that consciousness has to pop out of the notion of you as the person, and pop into itself as consciousness.

What does it mean to empty the mind?

It means to empty the pockets of your mind by not identifying with what is in them. To turn them inside out and let it all drop from your grasp while you remain as pure conscious awareness.

Is it normal to feel spiritually alone?

Aloneness can be healthy in the right context. It is unhealthy when it is the ego feeling lonely, rejected, isolated, or passively hostile in some way. Essence, on the other hand, can be quite happy by itself while still being accepting of others. Some body types and essences even prefer being by themselves and this is normal. The only thing that corrupts the normalcy of aloneness is the negativity of the ego. Another thing to be on guard against is feeling spiritually superior and aloof and judgmental of others who are not inclined the same way. The more spiritually advanced you are, the more you will embrace all of life and existence as cherished manifestations and expressions of creation.

Why do some spiritual groups seem to withdraw and isolate themselves?

You have to see this in historical context because spiritual ideas throughout history have contradicted religious beliefs and laws as well as political philosophies. People who were interested in spiritual ideas had to be discreet which led to secret societies, exclusive schools, and so on. It is also true that not everyone can be interested in or prepared to take these ideas the right way—as a door to inner transformation and not simply a means for becoming a better person. These things are still true, yet we live in an age where spirituality has become popularized around the globe, so there is more openness and less opposition. Nevertheless, some groups have held onto the idea that they need to be exclusive and secretive, and they promote this within their organizations. It is also true that these ideas naturally exclude people who are not interested in them and in times like now we don't have to hide or disguise them, and we don't have to hide or disguise our interest in them. Spiritual truth inherently leads not to increasing isolation but to a realization of the unity of life. They do not exclude. They include and embrace and allow.

But isn't there value in isolation?

It depends on what you mean. In most cases, isolation—which comes from the meaning of insulation—is a form of protection that usually involves withdrawal and removal. You even see this in the idea of winning a competition which becomes a celebration of 'my' uniqueness at the expense of the defeat and humiliation and even destruction of your ego. My ego must isolate itself from yours and yours from mine to signal victory and defeat. Competitions are now replete with primal screams, negative glares at the opponent, an attempt to spite or humiliate the opponent, and a sense of hostility toward the 'enemy' competitor. Most sporting events wreak of this kind of psychological violence and yet the public celebrates it, considers it normal, and passes it on to children who eagerly adopt it as part of the display and armor of their ego. All of this is far removed from the simplicity and tenderness of essence and the purity of awareness.

Isolation also seems to reinforce depression...

In fact, they reinforce each other. Depression, even in severe and ostensibly justifiable situations, is a negative manifestation and expression of the ego. The instinctive center is unhappy about something and the ego is associating with that, identifying with that, and exhibiting that. Depression is usually multilayered, but at the root you will find the instinctive center if you know how to look. But it is not easy because you have to look through and beyond the ego to see this root and to see how the ego is clinging to it. Animals can also suffer extreme abuse and neglect, which may affect their energy and behavior, but they never get depressed as such because they don't have an ego.

Depression is now a very common social ill…

    Social illnesses are psychological illnesses. And like instinctive illnesses, they stem from a lack of circulation, free exchange, and connectedness to the whole. In the physical body, a lack of circulation or blocked circulation leads to a corruption of cells that starts to destroy some or all of the rest of the body. In human society the same thing manifests as conflict, confrontation, physical fighting, and war. The most commonly sought solution to these is another version of the same thing, and death ensues: not only the death of people, but of societies, educational institutions, cultures, and civilizations. And what is least understood is that this is what is *supposed* to happen within the fabric of humanity as part of the larger mechanism of organic life on earth in the solar system. It is why the fourth way regards organic life on earth as the stomach of the solar system. Things are being mashed and churned. Some ingredients are being distilled to fortify the mind and body. Others get eliminated.

But even as we are seeing more depression in people we are also seeing more people living in the moment. Isn't this a good sign?

It may be. It may also be that this has become a fashionable idea which is not properly understood. For instance, we talk about the moment as though it is a point in time, but it is not a point and it is not in time. That is just how the mind conceives of it and expresses it. In reality—which means from the perspective of conscious awareness—the past, the present, and the future are all one and nothing at the same time. Conscious existence is not fragmented or sequential or measurable. It simply *is*. I know you have heard this before and I know it can come across as spiritual arrogance or nonsense, but it is true. The mind and body and ego view things through the lens of time and space, but that is a limited lens and not the only lens available. So instead of thinking in terms of living in the moment maybe it is more accurate to think in terms of living as consciousness in awareness. From there what we call the moment starts to look very different.

What do you mean that all questions are not the same?

I mean the intent behind them. Before you pose a question, try to notice the tone of intent. Is it genuine? Is it just curiosity? Or is your ego wanting to pull the other person's ego into an arena where it can show off, oppose, challenge, and compete?

Why do we fall into identification so easily?

Partly because it is a habit, partly because we like it, and most of all because it is supposed to be that way. It is a universal law that governs unconscious human beings. Sometimes you can feel the energy of consciousness pouring into one or more centers with a certain ferocity. To someone who does not know about identification, this can feel good. For those who do know, it becomes unpleasant and disappointing to find that we have again fallen into the lake of identification. We look for the ladder of awareness to swim to as soon as we can.

How can I see my center of gravity?

When you walk through a neighborhood at night you may see a house where the lights are on just on one floor. The rest of the house is dark. You can see the same thing in yourself and in other people, and it is usually because of center of gravity. Most if not all the psychic energy is being spent on and expended from primarily one center. Try to notice whether you are preoccupied mainly with thoughts and ideas, or feelings and relationships, or projects and accomplishments, or health and physique. Don't rush to a conclusion. Just keep observing yourself in this way. It also helps to ask other people, but for this they usually have to be interested in these ideas.

What does it mean that the flame of enlightenment can be transmitted directly?

If you lean an unlit candle into the flame of a burning candle, it will ignite. If you place a static cello near one that is being plucked, the strings on the static cello will start to vibrate. This is transmission. It can happen between people, but it can also happen when you read something potent or hear certain music or perceive from a heightened emotion. Something crosses over and crosses beyond, which is what 'trans-mit' means. But it does not cross *from* person to person. It is a transmission of awareness to awareness, or to the seed of awareness.

In my case thinking feels very productive and it gives me a solid foundation that I see no need to abandon. Is this a problem?

It depends. Thoughts are reactions, reflections, and byproducts of perception. This byproduct can serve as useful material for the mind It can also spawn additional thoughts that are not useful. For example, the mind can shovel ideas all day long without leading anywhere. The question is, where is your thinking leading? Is it leading you toward conscious awareness or just into more thinking?

Why is it so uncomfortable to hear the truth about myself?

Try to look more carefully at who or what feels

uncomfortable when it is exposed. This feeling is lodged in the emotional center and the instinctive center and the intellectual center and pulling up its roots in all three is painful. Your question could also be stated as, "Why is it so uncomfortable to hear the truth about my imaginary picture of myself?" Here is a hint: the discomfort you feel is a camouflage; hiding behind it is the sense of 'I'. Try to look past the discomfort and see if you can get a glimpse of 'I'. The more clearly you see *that*, the more your observation of it will transmute as conscious awareness.

So just look without judging myself?

Look without judging your imaginary picture of yourself, because judgment is part of that image of 'me', part of the camouflage. Everything you can perceive in the internal and the external world has some kind of form. Keep looking behind the *form* of everything. Look behind the feeling of 'I'. Look behind the judgment. Look behind all negative emotions. Look behind sensations, thoughts, feelings. other people's egos. Behind events, politics, war, the stock market. Look behind your idea of the future and your interpretation of the past. Hurl the spear of awareness all the way through *everything* until you reach the other side of everything.

Can the mind at some point reconcile reality?

As you see deeper into the void of being, the mind adjusts its concepts of reality, but it can never *see* reality. What it reconciles is its idea of reality. This can quiet the mind and give it comfort, but it is not reality itself.

Can you say more about the forms in the inner world?

For example, thoughts are forms. Emotions are forms. Sensations are forms. They are all the same energy forming itself and taking shape at different levels of speed and density. What is so interesting about our inner world is that it is invisible to the human eye, yet consciousness can see it. Gradually you realize that this fact is far more interesting than the forms you see.

I often feel weighed down by the sense that I can't awaken.

The 'I' asking the question *imagines* that it can or cannot awaken, but neither of those 'I's or any other 'I' awakens. At the same time almost everyone gets stuck there in some form and struggles from there until one day we see that it is just an image in the mind, that we as consciousness are stuck in an image, and that we are not even stuck because there is nothing to be stuck in. When that 'I' pronounces itself as a thought or feeling or both, try to use it is a catalyst, a reminder, a launching pad to realize yourself as consciousness seeing it.

What is the best antidote to confusion?

Consciousness is never confused. When it identifies, it collapses into the mind and then the mind gets confused. Confusion is a reflex; a sort of agitation in the intellectual center caused by the intellectual center's inability to clearly sort and organize ideas or information. The result is that it jams and this jamming affects the emotional center which wants resolution. At that point you have the negative emotion of irritation and frustration, and the first step for getting out of it is to see it and not identify with it. Sometimes this will clear up the confusion, and sometimes you just have to wait for the intellectual center to clear itself out before pursuing whatever topic had led to the confusion. But the important thing is to realize that consciousness doesn't have to identify with the confusion and turn it into a problem. Just wait. As Lao Tzu said, "Do you have the patience to wait until your mud settles and the water is clear?"

The fourth way refers to god as the absolute. Is it suggesting that god is just a concept?

Everything is a concept for the intellectual center which interpolates all information as a concept, as well as for the emotional center which conceives things in the form of beliefs. Neither of these centers can fathom the primordial source of being which spawns awareness and gives rise to creation as the universe. Calling it the 'absolute' is the system's way of suggesting that there is something far more real than the image of a god, and that this reality is the sacred mystery of all mysteries.

In terms of being conducive to awakening, is it better to live in the country than in the city?

Not necessarily. Cities and towns are interesting organisms. Take away the word 'city' and envision a large organism pulsating as a mix of energies and forms in constant motion. Cities are not unlike galaxies and humans are not unlike solar systems sweeping through them every day, returning to their point of origin, and then sweeping through them again and again, day after day. Granted, there are more distractions to self-remembering in a city, but that can be a good thing, a good test of the consciousness of awareness.

How does our center of gravity come into play in terms of helping and hindering us?

Each of the four centers molds *its pattern* of reality into a form it can understand. The ego then takes up a position of security in whichever center is most predominant. Each person starts their search for the truth from this stronghold, through this lens. It is also the meaning behind the three traditional ways or paths to enlightenment: the instinctive-moving way of the fakir, the emotional way of the monk, and the intellectual way of the yogi. The fourth way is about walking all three paths simultaneously and approaching the truth through all the centers in a balanced way.

How will we know when we come into touch with pure being?

Pure being refers to the source behind awareness, the conscious beingness from which awareness springs and which is conscious *as* itself without having to be aware *of* anything else. It belongs to itself as the source of itself. The four centers cannot come into contact with this source, but awareness can. It is the penultimate expansion of the self-realization of conscious awareness.

Where does the impulse to search for our real self come from?

It comes as a reflection from pure being itself, but we usually experience it as a combination of thought and emotion that compels us toward the truth.

Why do you refer to pure being as the void?

Because it is beyond emptiness, beyond stillness, beyond silence, beyond all palpability by the body, mind, and emotions. In comparison to all these things it is like a void. At the same time it is more full and complete than all of them combined. But it is hard to get at the exact description with words.

Does the fear of death also come from pure being?

The fear of death comes from the four centers. There is no fear in pure being because it has no mechanism for perceiving in terms of fear. Look closely and you will see that the body and mind conspire together to create what we call fear. It is also interesting to remove the word 'fear' and examine the phenomenon itself? What do you see? As you look at it, realize that you can see it manifesting in you. How is this possible? How can you see it? What is seeing the thing called fear? Go more and more in that direction and see what you discover.

Is it a matter of having a right attitude toward death?

The person—the mind—can develop clear and positive attitudes about death, but the person and mind do not survive death. They both cease to operate and eventually cease to exist. The ego they housed vanishes along with them because it was just an image they were projecting inside themselves. So we want more than a positive attitude about death. We want to knowingly transcend death as the pure consciousness of awareness. But an attitude can help in the sense of preparing us for the reality that we have to let everything go, including and starting with our imaginary sense of 'I' as a person. To fully transcend the fear of death, we have to transcend 'I'.

What is behind our resistance to things?

We don't like pressure in any of the centers. It is uncomfortable. That is really what discomfort means: pressure. The word resist means 'to stand against' which is what the four centers and the ego do in response to pressure. Try to observe the difference in the energy inside when you resist versus when you do not resist pressure as it comes. What is the difference when you identify with pressure compared to when you do not identify with it?

What difference do you see?

There is more than one difference, but one of the most important is the resulting energy. When we identify, it produces a negative charge; when we remain conscious it starts to produce a neutral charge. But for that we have to consciously bear the pressure long enough for the charge to switch from negative to neutral. It is precisely what we are trying to do in relation to negative emotions so as to transform the energy—the pressure—behind them.

In both cases, the key point is that we are not trying simply to resolve the pressure and feel better. We are trying to consciously transmute the energy inside the pressure and created by the pressure. We cannot do this if we are identified.

Are you opposed to electronic devices?

Not in themselves, only in the effect they have. Technology has become an electronic extension of the ego in the sense that it gives the ego an added dimension with which to project and fuel itself. For example, the phone enables the ego to interact with other egos at great distances. Then when people meet in person they find it difficult to interact in the normal human way. A conflict arises between the physical and the electronic self. The way you imagine yourself via technology contradicts the way you imagine yourself in person, and this foments psychological problems, especially in the minds of young people whose identity is not yet fully formed and settled. They start to have a harder time than usual understanding who they are. As a result their emotional centers run amok and their personalities start to adopt distortions of reaction and behavior.

What is your position on karma?

The common idea of karma suggests that you as a person and the mind as a mind can reincarnate based on a cumulative result of decisions, deeds, and actions. But it does not take into account that consciousness is independent of the mind and body. So does karma mean that consciousness will reincarnate along with the mind and body, or in another mind and body with the karmic history of the previous mind and body? Does it also imply some kind of punishment for consciousness; that it needs to rectify and balance something in the next mind and body? And what happens if it succeeds or fails? You can see how this idea shares things in common with religions which state that believers will go to heaven while non-believers will go to hell. With both karma and religion, the emphasis is on behavior and action and morality *as a person.* An inner meaning of karma is that the more consciously aware you are now, the more conscious awareness will become, which means the reverse is also true.

Will my life change as I become more aware?

Your life circumstances may not change much. But the more the realization of awareness deepens and expands, the more your life as a person will seem unreal, illusory, dream-like. You will find yourself waking up *in* the dream of your life but the dream will not change. Not until you wake up *from* the dream does it start to change the nature of the dream. Because then you will be outside it in a different dimension and no longer identified with it.

Why does the process of awakening seem so confounding sometimes?

There is a door between the mind and pure consciousness. Awareness keeps passing back and forth through this door. All our talk is about what is on the other side of the door, but the mind keeps trying to understand it in terms of its experience on this side of the door, which leads to distortion and confusion. This is normal and in a way necessary because consciousness has to eventually let go of the mind and rise above it. Which is also tricky because confusion can turn into a compulsion of needing to know the unknowable and then we feel we must reconcile the two. But it is not true. We can just let go of our confoundment and float above it. It is an option that most people rarely consider.

My thoughts seem like good allies. I find it hard to disassociate with them.

You don't need to disassociate with them. You just need to realize they are thoughts, and that they are not what is conscious of them. Try to notice that you can see them but they cannot see you noticing them. As they wander out of the house on errands of thinking, give them as long a leash as you want to, but keep the source of their attention at home.

~ ~ ~

The Silent Self

'I' and Consciousness

Whoever knows himself knows god.
Muhammad

IT IS IMPORTANT to know what you mean when you say 'I' because you may mean the 'I' of consciousness or the 'I' of ego. Self-observation and self-investigation mean exploring both to discover *what you are not* as the identity of a person, and *what you are* as pure consciousness.

Are essence and personality also different dimensions?

Yes, in the sense that they are different dimensions in and through which consciousness manifests. Essence is a higher, finer, lighter dimension. Personality is lower, denser, heavier dimension. Negative emotions are even more dense and more heavy. And conscious awareness is the lightest and purest of all. The model of the ray of creation in the fourth way system enunciates these distinctions. It gives you a clear map with which to comprehend the mechanical dissolution and conscious resolution of the fundamental substance comprising the universe. There are not many maps like this.

The fourth way also talks about food, air, and impressions. How do they affect awareness?

The head, chest, and abdomen are the three 'stories' of the human machine as described in the fourth way. The abdomen absorbs food. The chest absorbs air. The mind absorbs impressions of light and sound. Each of these 'foods' *enters* through our head—through the mouth, the nose, and the eyes and ears. From there they settle into their respective sections of the body to be absorbed. The idea is that three kinds of matter get distilled in different stories, but only up to a point that serves survival and procreation. To be further distilled, their energy needs to be mixed with consciousness itself. This is particularly true of the impressions of sound and even more of light because whereas the body automatically distills food and air, it barely registers impressions of sight and sound. These impressions can be absorbed far more consciously if we know how to add the influence of consciousness itself.

You mean self-remembering?

Yes. For instance, as you look at me and listen to me, notice that you can be aware of looking and listening. Notice that you can be aware behind your eyes and inside your ears. Normally we leave our perch inside, go out to meet what we see or hear, and then cling to it. We do the same thing with our thoughts and emotions and bodily sensations. Self-remembering refers to consciousness staying in its perch and realizing it is staying here. This has many nuances that you have to discover for yourself, but this is how it begins.

Why do we feel the need to be liked and admired?

Essence wants to be nurtured, but not for the sake of identity. It wants to be nurtured so as to be cultivated as the seedcase of consciousness. There is an innate wish, you could say, to become more of what it is as the potential of consciousness. But very quickly, due to its tendency to become identified, essence starts to conceive of itself *in relation to* other people and from there it forms as a sense of identity that learns to insulate itself with increasing layers of identity. As this happens, our innate *wish* to be nurtured as what we really are as essence turns into a *need* to be paid attention to, accepted, liked, and admired as a person and personality. And in most cases, the hurt we feel when our needs are not met is a reaction of personality. Deep inside the insulation of personality, the core of essence is usually fine. It is just asleep, dormant. And the truth is that essence itself never needed to be admired or liked. That is not what the true nature of essence is about.

Is it necessary to trench down through all the layers of insulation in our personality to rediscover ourselves as essence?

That is the approach of psychotherapy, and it has validity. What is often missing in that approach, however, is the understanding that personality and essence are different dimensions of being. They don't exist on equal ground or in the same form. This is why the fourth way emphasizes the non-expression of negative emotions because non-expression is meant to neutralize the grip that personality has over essence and to loosen the soil in which essence is meant to sprout. Three other things that nurture essence are beauty, friendship, and truth. A fourth is real suffering because the force of suffering is the most potent agent for dissolving the layers of personality and strengthening essence. This may sound contrary to the delicate nature of essence, but it is true because essence is a different dimension than personality. Essence is surprisingly more resilient and adaptable than personality, especially in the face of suffering.

What is the difference right now between my awareness and yours?

The only distinction may be the degree to which it knows it is here as the consciousness of awareness. This is not the feeling of being the person of you or the person of me. And it is not the feeling of 'I' inside either of us. Just beyond all of these, consciousness is quietly and gently watching us ask and answer this question.

Many teachings talk about everything as an illusion, yet here we are. How do you explain the paradox?

The paradox is due to thinking in terms of opposites: that either everything is real or everything is an illusion. The intellectual center usually stops there, but it can go farther. It cannot, however, go as far as consciousness which has a more comprehensive perspective that includes different dimensions of reality. From this perspective, it is seen that each dimension appears a certain way *to itself* in its dimension. But things look different from a higher dimension. It is not that they don't exist, but that they no longer appear to be what they had seemed in the lower dimension. For example, in the second state people appear to be 'real' identities with personal problems. From the third state you see that everyone is caught up in the notion of being a person; that their consciousness is enshrouded in a mental image that is experiencing life and identity as 'I'. In the fourth state, all of it appears as a projection. If consciousness rises high enough, there is the realization that the pure being of consciousness is projecting an image—a dream—of itself in *the form* of the universe. Inside this dream of itself as the universe, it projects a further dream of itself in *the form* of objects in the universe, including the object of being an individual person with a unique identity. And inside the dream of being this person it projects images of itself in *the form of* psychological daydreams as well as night dreams. Meanwhile, each lower dimension cannot see that it is a projection *within* the dimension above it, which in turn is a projection of the next dimension above it—all the way back to the original source of all of them. At that point, everything is an illusory projection of the same source in which everything is one.

Is it the ego that prevents us from realizing this?

From one point of view, yes. From another point of view, the ego is simply a *result* of what prevents this realization. In our normal state of consciousness, we unwittingly cling to *what* we perceive and to *what* we feel at the expense of perception realizing itself as perception. Rarely do we turn the light of awareness around onto itself, to the source of itself which is not dependent on the perception *of* anything. This is what the fourth way means by self-remembering, and it is actually the most interesting thing about awareness—not *what* it is aware *of* through perception, but the nature of itself as *the source of perceiving*. The process of ascending into higher and higher dimensions of consciousness is based on this.

How important is memory?

Memory is mind activity. It is not awareness. It is a record in the mind of what awareness has perceived. It is the photograph that was developed in the dark room of each of the four centers as a result of the light of consciousness being cast through them during your life. The image retained in the memory banks of the four centers is not 'you'. It is simply an image of you as a person. The real 'you' is the light behind. It is simply here perceiving. This light does not retain memory of itself and does not leave any trace of itself.

Is eternity just the long line of time stretched out?

Eternity is neither time nor an endless extension of time. That is how the mind views it. Time exists in the mind as a contrivance of the mind. Eternity is the uncontrived absence of time and of space.

Sometimes it feels strange to be human…

The human being is a complex form of creation.

It may be one of the most complex creations in the universe because designed into it is the possibility for consciousness to realize itself. When you stop and think about this it is indeed strange.

Do you think we somehow choose to become human?

It seems that each human being is a temptation of form which pure consciousness has a hard time not identifying with. The pull toward *identity in form* is very strong because it is a universal law. Some teachings say that it is consciousness playing with itself in a form of hide and seek. The thing we want to understand, however, is that transformation implies consciousness escaping from identification by reversing the magnetism—the direction of flow—such that consciousness draws itself back into the source of itself, and that this is also something it chooses to do.

Do you believe in the 'big bang' theory?

The big bang theory is a mind idea that is limited to one dimension. For instance, an original 'thrust' would have to come from something and there is little or no evidence of what that might be. Even less understood is why it would happen and what it means in terms of different dimensions. So it is based primarily on supposition, albeit supposition derived from data about the universe expanding.

Maybe time and space emerged out of the big bang...

Time and space are mind concepts. In reality, time is not time and space is not space. The mind cannot grasp the truth of this. Even science cannot explain what is going on all around us and inside us.

And death?

Death is another mind idea that seems valid, yet it is based on the mind's idea of itself as an identity with a body. From one side, this idea is correct because the forms of the mind and body are not permanent. They perish and disintegrate. But this does not take into account what consciousness is. If you conclude that the body generates consciousness, then from that view consciousness also dies. Whereas if you conclude that the mind and body are a projection of consciousness into form, it means that death is the end of the form but not of the consciousness that projected it. And then there is the matter of the degree to which consciousness is conscious of itself or not. By virtue of being conscious as itself, maybe it changes the nature of itself as consciousness. Maybe it explodes in the opposite direction back into itself as the source of all creation. Maybe that's the *real* big bang.

The self and its thoughts seem intimately connected.

The self of awareness is not a self as such. It is not an identity that has thoughts. It is more accurate to say that the mind and its thoughts are connected, and that what connects them as a feeling of self is the image of 'I' produced *in the mind.* As you diminish identification with thoughts, you as consciousness see that thoughts are just reflections being pumped by the four centers into the psychological arena of the mind where they take center stage for a time and then dissipate and get replaced by new ones. The consciousness of all this is not in the arena—except when it forgets itself and becomes identified with thoughts as 'my' thoughts and as 'me' thinking.

Are the mind and the ego the same thing?

What we call the ego cannot exist without the mind because it is just a fabrication in the mind. Try to put your ego in your hand. The mind, however, can exist without the ego as simply a mechanism or tool without a sense of identity attached to it.

Is there a clear demarcation between the two?

What we call the mind is an instrument that converts perceptions of the reflections of light from phenomena into a psychological form that we call thought. Due to identification, consciousness transforms into a sense of self in relation to thoughts and amasses around them as a mental parasite. But consciousness can also realize that perception, reflections, and thoughts are not the same thing, and that it can see them all. It then realizes that it can transform itself back into itself.

Are you referring to essence?

Essence is simple awareness unaware of itself. It is consciousness unconscious of itself as consciousness. It perceives but does not know it is perceiving. So, yes, essence is what sees. What I was describing, however, is the result of essence consciously becoming aware of itself as perception—which is what self-remembering means. This is what the fourth way calls the first conscious shock. It is produced when the seed of essence 'opens' as conscious awareness.

How can I see that my life is a dream?

A dream does not seem like a dream when you are in it. Only when you wake up do you see that it was a dream. But even then you make the mistake of thinking 'I' was dreaming. In actuality, the feeling of 'I' is imposed on the background of pure being, and the dreams which 'I' has are imposed on the feeling of 'I'. They are dreams within the dream of 'I'. So first you have to step out of the dreams that 'I' is having. Then you have to step out of the dream of 'I' itself. You then see that, although there is a body and mind, your sense of identity in them is essentially a dream; a projection of an image of self based on identification with the body and mind. Waking up means consciousness extracting itself from identification with the forms it is projecting and escaping from identity in those forms.

Can an individual have significance in humanity?

Each human form is like a tiny corpuscle that fills up with the energy of pure being. What we usually think of as identity, as our self, is the corpuscle, the shell that has been filled up. That which has filled it up is not conscious of itself, but it can be. Otherwise *everyone* in humanity is playing an unconscious role in the larger scheme of earthly events in the solar system.

Does pure being impose identity onto us?

Pure being does not impose identity onto anyone or onto anything, or onto itself. It is the antithesis of identity. It is the spirit of reality.

Why doesn't pure being just exist for itself and leave it at that?

Perhaps to pure being all of creation is just breathing, which many eastern teachings allude to.

Why do we need thoughts?

We don't need thoughts to exist, but we do need them to communicate with other human beings. And according to the fourth way system, the moon needs them in the sense that we could not form an ego and negative emotions without them.

If humanity is asleep, how do you account for the fact that so many great things have been accomplished?

It all seems very impressive, and on its own level, in its own dimension, it is. Nevertheless, mankind throughout history has focused on what is seen rather than on what is seeing, yet this simple distinction has almost always gone unnoticed and been dismissed. The focus has always been on forms rather than on the formlessness of the reality behind form.

Is pure being the deepest sense of 'I am'?

The thought, feeling, and sensation of 'I am' is the result of a reflection in the mind of the perception of consciousness. Consciousness itself does not form as a sense of 'I'. So when you experience 'I am' in yourself, look just behind and beyond it. That is where you enter the dimension that leads to pure being.

Who is speaking the truth when we speak from our deepest being?

It depends on how deep you mean. For instance, you can develop a sincere part of your personality that values truth and the pursuit of reality, and it may express itself accordingly. Deeper than that may be a highly mature essence whose human expression manifests a great depth of experience, understanding, and suffering. Beyond that is the wordlessness of consciousness itself. And beyond all of them at the depth of all depths as their source is pure being.

What do you see as the largest obstacle or limitation of man number four?

Man number four is still caught up in the identity of seeking, of being a seeker or pupil who will find something or reach something. In other words, despite his or her earnestness and knowledge, man number four is still operating in the mind as the ego, even as a well meaning spiritual ego. Consciousness has not yet popped out of the notion of being a person who is working toward something.

Isn't the consciousness in each of us somehow unique?

Yes and no. The self-realization that occurs in all people is the same consciousness recognizing its being. In this sense it is not unique. It is not 'personal'. What is personal is the circumstances of the human being in whom the self-recognition of consciousness takes place. Although consciousness is formless, it recognizes itself—it reflects itself—within the form of a human being and this reflection is described as 'my' moment of awakening. But that is really the perspective of 'me' as a person. It is not consciousness itself. Consciousness is the formless realizing itself within form. And the form is temporary. It ultimately does not matter except perhaps in rare cases to give meaning to historical context. Otherwise it does not matter, and the 'story' of awakening that surrounded it does not matter. It is all part of the skin that is shed.

When you say historical context, do you mean self-realized spiritual masters and artists and so on?

Yes, their legacy remains for awhile in what we call history for history's sake and for the purposes of mankind. But it is only a legacy. A perfume. A memory. A trace of the form as a person. The pure being of consciousness is beyond all that.

But didn't they feel themselves as 'me'?

Beneath the layers of name, race, nationality, gender, religion, beliefs, cultural upbringing, profession, talents, and the rest there is a feeling of 'I' and 'me'. Yet this, too, is not inherent in pure being. It comes about as a result of the form—the formation—of the mind and body in which the ego is projected. If you could trace this sense of 'me' to its deepest root in the mind you would come to the same feeling of self in everyone. Just beyond that physiological, psychological notion of 'I' is pure consciousness which has no identity and does not experience itself as an identity of self. It simply *is* and knows that it is, and knows that it is not the human in whom it is temporarily embodied.

And yet the person knows they are enlightened, yes?

This is an interesting question. It may depend on

how conscious consciousness is and to what degree it 'knows' itself. It may be quite conscious and yet the mind does not know anything about this. On the other hand, the mind may be familiar with ideas about enlightenment and generate thoughts like 'I am enlightened' without it being true. It is never enough just to think about all these ideas.

The world seems to be headed toward catastrophe and even destruction. Does that concern you?

Despite what we think about it and read about it, the world is fine in a larger sense because it is part of a much larger reality than just itself. Take away all your information, attitudes, expectations, and beliefs and leave the world as just a layer of organic life, which includes humanity, wrapped around the surface of a planet that is much bigger than we are and under the influences of much bigger forces than we know about or can control. Consider, too, that the life of the earth is happening the same way your life is happening. You suffer about it all to the extent that you identify with it and imagine that you can control it and change it. When you remove *all* your identification, expectations, and hopes and remain fully conscious as you look at the world, the picture changes.

What about compassion for people, animals, and the environment?

You will find yourself beyond the world experiencing the compassion of compassion. As we are, we feel intense emotions, but as the realization of consciousness transforms our emotions, the perception they offered us gets superseded by pure perception and understanding of the whole. This includes a deeper perception and understanding of what suffering is and what it means for all forms of life.

Is that the meaning of, 'you shall know the truth and the truth shall set you free'?

Yes, although there is more to that statement. For instance, when the presumed person named Jesus said that to his disciples, he was not addressing their minds. He was addressing consciousness in them. He was sending a message to consciousness itself. That is what 'knows' the truth and is set free.

And the truth destroys fear and desires?

To a large extent, but not necessarily completely. It does not mean that the person ceases to have impulses of fear and desire. It means that these phenomena no longer taint consciousness. Consciousness remains beyond them watching them arise and circulate. At the same time, the presence of conscious awareness neutralizes fear and desire, so they can no longer operate with full identification. It is not fear and desire, but the identification behind them, that is the problem.

How does suffering give us energy?

In the case of real suffering, when you take away the identification—the clinging of consciousness—you are left with a force of energy acting on the mind and body without an ego as part of the equation. So it is not personal; it is just the suffering of pain or sorrow or loss. This energy, which is unique to the human form, can be powerful in two ways: it can fortify your sense of identity, or it can deepen the self-realization and self-liberation of conscious awareness. The determining factor is identification. This is not the explanation of a formula. It is something you come to within your being. But most people never come to this hidden potential of suffering, largely because they never penetrate beneath the feeling that it is personal. There is a rich, rare vein deep within real suffering, but only consciousness can tap it.

Don't you agree that science has made tremendous strides in understanding the universe?

The scientific view of the universe is that humans, the earth, the solar system, the galaxy, and beyond all exist in the same dimension. According to the fourth way, they are separate dimensions that encompass and are encompassed by other dimensions. This means that space and time are not the same throughout the universe. The scientific view—which, remember, is a product of the human mind—also cannot account for the reality of a conscious source beyond all form, all space, all time, all dimensions. Science has nothing with which to detect or measure that.

When I meditate, I try to float in the stillness between thoughts, but the thoughts themselves don't necessarily quiet down. What do you suggest?

The framework—the structure—of the mind is silent. Only its contents are noisy. Meditation at its best is about transcending all thought with the purpose of attuning the *structure* of the mind. The influence of conscious awareness directed at the structure calms down this structure which in turn calms down the pumping of thoughts and emotions. Ideally, yoga is meant to have the same effect on the *structure of the body* and in turn on sensations *in* the body. Something else to consider is that the 'I' you describe as a deeper sense of yourself floating is just another 'I' that is trying to float above all its colleagues. This 'I', too, has to be transcended. When it is you will have a different relationship to meditation.

Can you help me find my way through this painful suffering (from a woman who was going through a period of severe anguish)?

Real human suffering is a spiritual dish that is an acquired taste. When it is served to us the best route is to be silent, not complain or feel sorry for ourselves, and to be as conscious as we can while allowing the force of suffering to pass all the way through our being, and to not talk too much about it afterwards. Profound suffering can lead to profound transformation when we navigate its waters as conscious awareness.

Sort of like being in the background as the screen of awareness?

You can think of it like that, but remember that the word background is just a word. It is just an image for the mind to relate to. A background still exists as an object inside space whereas consciousness is not an object. It is more like the entire field of space. It surrounds suffering while at the same time penetrating to the core of suffering.

Imagination also plays out on the background screen, doesn't it?

Yes. Imagination starts as a projection of the reflections of perception. We perceive something and our perceptions get reflected in the mind as associative images and thoughts. Consciousness then identifies with them and loses itself in their stream. Sometimes the current in this stream is slight, sometimes it is extreme, depending on the degree of identification. When you see it clearly, you see that imagination is a very strange thing because it represents consciousness projecting itself into the psychological world and creating itself there in the form of images. It is like the light in the projector looking for itself by projecting itself through the image of the film and onto the mind as a vague sense of 'I'. In this sense, imagination is not bad. It is simply a misdirection. In the biblical sense, it is consciousness 'missing the mark' which is what the word 'sin' means. The mark it is missing is the pure presence of itself as the source of all projection. Instead of realizing this, it gets caught up in the distraction and entertainment of its own projection. Also, what the fourth way calls imagination is what we usually call daydreaming, but it has many more facets than that because your body can be driving or eating or talking or making love while at the same time consciousness is lost deep in imagination.

Do you think it helps to do a combination of meditation and yoga?

It is really a personal choice. What is more important to understand is why you are doing them. Ultimately, their purpose is to promote—to free— the circulation of consciousness in the centers. Meditation is designed to free consciousness in the intellectual center, yoga is designed to free it in the moving center, prayer is designed to free it in the emotional center, and chanting and drumming are designed to free it in the instinctive center. The idea is that if you free the circulation of consciousness in one center it will promote circulation in the other centers such that consciousness will recognize *itself* above all the centers. Freeing consciousness *within* the centers opens the door for it to free itself as self-realization *above* the centers.

It feels like the deeper I go into my psychological world the more easy it is to get distracted. Is there an antidote for this?

Our teacher used to say, "You are not what you observe. You are the observer." This simple statement is true at every dimension of consciousness. If you hold to this truth, you will successfully navigate all the depths of the void. It also hints as to why self-observation and self-remembering have to go together to be effective and keep you on track.

Why is it helpful to notice the gaps between thoughts?

What seem like gaps or empty spaces to the mind are in fact gulfs of consciousness. We usually hurry across these gulfs as soon as possible rather than allow ourselves to fall into them—into the depths of presence. What we call moments of awkward silence are really deep pools of consciousness waiting for us to plunge into them.

Can you talk about the difference between thoughts and emotions?

They are both like mirrors that reflect the perceptions of consciousness. Thoughts are reflections in the intellectual center. Emotions are reflections in the emotional center. The emotional center is faster so it renders these reflections in ethereal form whereas the intellectual center, which responds more slowly, interpolates perceptions in a more solid form which we experience as concepts, labels, principles, rules, definitions. Emotions can flush in the chest and face like a heat wave. Thoughts form strictly in the head with little or no physical sensation attached to them.

Is the universe the mind of god?

The mind and the universe are similar in that both are filled with objects which circulate and ricochet inside them. In both, everything has its place and form, and the whole is both orderly and chaotic. We might also say that the universe is the mind of a much higher dimension of consciousness, and that the human mind is a smaller universe in which the same consciousness is projecting itself.

Should we feel an urgency that there is no time to lose?

On one level, yes. But that is an interesting expression—"there is no time to lose"—because it is also true in pure being where there is no time.

Can you say again about emotions being faster than thoughts?

The emotional center operates at a much faster speed of response than the intellectual thoughts. This fact is hidden in the expression that 'a picture is worth more than a thousand words'. Emotions, due to their speed, reside between a flash of perception and the much slower formation of thought in response to the perception. Emotions lag behind perception, yet they precede and outpace thought. You could say that they are consciousness taking initial psychological form before taking secondary form as thought.

Knowledge is also thought, as opposed to knowledge being emotion.

This is worth investigating. What is knowledge? What is information? What purpose does it serve? What does our mind do with it? What happens after that? Is that the end of the matter? And what about understanding? Is that strictly intellectual or can it also be emotional, and if it is also emotional can it possibly be deeper than thought? This is rich material for self-observation.

Should we help others as much as we can?

Certainly. We must also know who in us is helping who in others. Persons helping other persons and helping each other is one thing. Conscious awareness arousing and reinforcing itself in others is another. Who are we when we help? And what sort of help? And why?

~ ~ ~

The Silent Self

Understanding Negative Emotions

Those who pass this barrier
walk freely throughout the universe.

the Mumon-kan

NEGATIVE EMOTIONS are chemical byproducts of the mind and the body. The body provides the raw material of negative energy. The mind provides the rational that allows this energy to gather in psychological form. These two ingredients, impelled by the force of identification, produce either a deep implosion or a violent explosion, or both. To fully understand what negative emotions are, we have to see all the way to their source, how they develop from this source, and how they help to shape and sustain the ego.

How can I overcome the tendency to criticize other people and myself?

Keep noticing how this tendency, which is a form of judgment, is a filter obscuring your view. Try to refrain from overcoming it. Try instead to see the feeling in you where this tendency is coming from. The more you see what is behind it, the more it will dissipate.

What is behind it?

An imaginary idea of yourself as a person who exists in relation to other people who, ironically, are caught up in the same imaginary loop. Judgment is really just egos weighing the pros and cons of egos in relation to themselves so as to feel legitimate as a sense of 'I'.

Why is it so hard to stop it?

Because you not only have to step out of the judgment; you have to step out of the entire notion of 'I'. Only consciousness can step all the way out.

How do we convert negative emotions into positive emotions?

Transformation is not a change that takes place in the mind. It is a crossing over from the dimension of mind into the dimension of consciousness. The word 'negative' comes from 'negare' which means to negate or deny. The word 'positive' comes from 'posit' which means to place or position. Whereas negative emotions negate reality, positive emotions arise from the position of seeing reality.

Negative emotions are a reactionary byproduct of the mind while positive emotions are a reflection of pure perception in the moment. You simply see the place—the actuality—of things as they are. You adapt and respond without resistance, and you perceive directly. What is interesting is that this leaves no room for an identity moving through time. In the present there is just living. Just *being* now in the midst of whatever is happening.

Another distinction is that negative emotions operate on the mind's false assumption that we can choose and change things, whereas positive emotions spring from awareness which simply sees things as they are. Positive emotions do not mean you are cheerful in unpleasant circumstances. It means you see the reality of what is happening.

Can we rationalize our way out of negativity?

You can rationalize your way out of the thinking that supports a negative emotion, but that is not always the full solution because the core of 'I' may still remain intact. The idea behind your question seems reasonable, but it assumes that negative emotions are transformed on the same level that they originate and manifest on, which is not the case. You cannot reason with or resolve a negative emotion in yourself or in another person and expect long-term change. For that you have to go above it, and only awareness can do that by not identifying with the projection of 'I' behind the negative emotion. You can prepare for transformation with the intellect, and that is useful, yet true transformation is not psychological work. It is a transcendence of consciousness that evaporates the sense of 'I' and frees the energy behind the negative emotion.

Can you say more about how not expressing negative emotions contains their energy and what to do next?

The idea is that you can either lose the energy of a negative emotion by expressing it, or contain that energy by not expressing it. But containing it does not mean just holding onto it. It means using the energy—the intensity—of the negative emotion as leverage to 'lift' consciousness out of the feeling of 'I' that is negative. You cannot do this if you are identified with the negative emotion. So consciousness has to unlock, unbind, un-attach itself from the feeling of 'I' and step out of the identity of 'I'.

But this is not a mental effort. You have to find the key to this next step for yourself. No one else can turn this key for you. It is what the fourth way calls the 'second conscious shock'. It has to come from deep inside. Deep beyond the sense of 'I'. It is not an effort in the usual sense, and it is not a feeling of 'I' am stepping out of 'my' feeling of identity. It is the *influence* of consciousness being aware of itself and knowing itself as pure perception in a different dimension.

You say that negative emotions negate reality. What do positive emotions do?

They don't really do anything. It is more that they absorb reality. They do not necessarily make you feel better or feel 'positive'. They come as a result of seeing reality as it is and affirming the truth of things. What is important to understand is that positive emotions are not the opposite of negative emotions. Negative emotions stem from the instinctive center and the ego. Positive emotions stem from conscious awareness. It is hard to even call them emotions. They are more like reflections of awareness that echo in the emotional center in pure form and have nothing to do with the ego.

Negative emotions are also not really emotions. They are *reactions*. For example, when you are negative you are reacting to something you don't like. Behind this reaction is a feeling of 'I' and 'me' that is trying to protect and defend itself. Positive emotions are very different. They are *reflections* of the openness and expansion of the pure seeing of conscious awareness.

What makes transformation possible?

Transformation is not possible as long as consciousness is entrenched in the feeling of 'I'. Transformation occurs as a result of consciousness seeing 'I', realizing it is seeing it, and realizing itself as the seeing. This realization occurs in relation to 'I', to negative emotions, to suffering, to everything.

What does the transformation of negative emotions give you?

It clarifies awareness. Awareness comes into more conscious focus. It does this by distilling a very fine energy out of the dense material of negative emotions. Another way to say it is that consciousness uses the pressure of that energy as lift, and it rises.

By dropping the negative emotion?

Not exactly. You don't drop the negative emotion. You drop identification with 'I'. When that happens the negative emotion releases the energy inside it. This energy is very special. When it gets released *inwardly* via non-identification, it fuels awareness. When it gets expressed *outwardly* through the centers, it fuels the ego. This difference is useful to think about and to examine in yourself.

How can I drop identification with 'I'? Is there a special effort for this?

To be able to drop 'I', consciousness has to recognize itself beyond 'I', outside of 'I'. It is also true that dropping identification with 'I' clarifies the realization that consciousness is already beyond 'I'. But you have to realize that 'I' cannot drop 'I'. Trying to do that means that consciousness is still entrenched in the feeling of you as a person trying to drop 'I'. Non-identification means consciousness stepping out of this sense of identity.

Is this related to the ingredients of si 12 and mi 12 that the food diagram talks about?

For those who don't know, these are fourth way terms related to the chemical explanation of transformation. The short answer is that si 12 is sex energy manifesting through the instinctive center from which negative emotions originate, while mi 12 is the intensity of vibration within the *current* of identification. When you change this vibration, transformation occurs. But this is not something the mind or body can do. It is not an effort of that kind. It is a 'shock' from consciousness itself, provided by the awareness of consciousness. You have to come to an intuitive realization of it and how it comes. And getting there is not necessarily pleasant. Transforming intense negative emotions can be difficult to bear because you are dealing with the raw material out of which a negative emotion has formed in the first place.

Is it a culmination of the first and second conscious shocks?

What the fourth way calls the first conscious shock of self-remembering refers to awareness establishing itself consciously; realizing its position as awareness. The second conscious shock of transformation refers to awareness consciously manifesting its influence over a negative emotion by seeing *through* the feeling of 'I' and accessing the energy *behind* the negative emotion. This is a technical description of the process, but it is not a step-by-step formula. It is simply how the mind might view it. In actuality it is an instantaneous transcendence, transformation, and transmutation of energy and perception. It occurs within a higher dimension of consciousness. The mind is not involved.

Any other hints or suggestions?

You can think of it like this: a negative emotion is like an atom comprising protons, neutrons, and electrons, but without a nucleus they cannot form as an atom. Non-identification dissolves the nucleus of 'I' which in turn releases all the energy back to the source it originally came from, which is consciousness itself. But you have to understand that we are talking about very powerful energies. In fact, deep *transmutation* of negative emotions and real suffering is far more powerful than the violent or intense *expression* of negative emotions.

Rodney Collin talked about matter in a molecular state and matter in an electronic state. Is this related?

You could say that self-remembering is the control of matter in molecular state and that the transformation of negative emotions (and suffering) is the control of matter in electronic state. But calling it control is not quite right. It is more accurate to call it the self-realization of consciousness in molecular form and the self-realization of consciousness in electronic form, which implies that awareness expands, which is true because the two conscious shocks refer to different dimensions. Consciousness extracts itself from the *psychological* dimension of thought and emotion as a higher and faster *molecular* dimension of awareness, and again as an even higher and faster *electronic* dimension of pure consciousness. Discovering the miraculous means discovering higher dimensions in your being.

Is the goal to get rid of negative emotions?

Not necessarily. As long as they emerge we want to absorb the energy inside them so as to transmute that energy as heightened consciousness. Under the light of consciousness they will at a certain point rid themselves of themselves and cease to emerge, or at least emerge less often and with less insistence. This means you no longer need them to draw energy from. It means you have exhausted that resource and need to find new, better resources.

Why would they continue to emerge?

It is better to say that some of their raw material would still emerge, but without identification it would not be able to take full shape as a negative emotion. For example, you might still stub your toe which would give rise to irritation, but it would flare simply as pain. It would not correlate to the feeling of 'I'.

So we could call them simply unpleasant emotions?

We could call them reactive emotions because when they surface it is a signal that something is being reacted to, usually in the form of resistance or rejection or denial. It is a defensive posture coming from our notion of 'I' and it is negatively charged because it stems from the negative half of the instinctive center. Examine a negative emotion closely and you will see that it is avoiding reality by trying to hide from something or push it away. Look behind this shield and you will find your imaginary picture of 'I'.

Isn't chief feature also behind negative emotions?

Yes, although this requires more knowledge and understanding. Chief feature is a mechanism that works in direct tandem with the instinctive center. It can be considered the chief tendency toward a specific kind of negative reaction. It is the chief 'handler' that passes negative energy from the instinctive center to the emotional center. Push someone into a corner, either physically or psychologically, and you will see chief feature flash through a predictable form of negative emotions. One type will fight back. Another will give up. Another will feel sorry for themselves. Another will panic. Another will roll up in a ball of resentment. Another will find it funny. What you are seeing is a combination of each person's body type, chief feature, and instinctive center reacting as an amalgam of 'I' behind their reaction.

So they go hand-in-hand with the ego?

They work hand in hand to shape your imaginary sense of 'I', but it all happens due to identification. Without identification, 'I' can't happen. The feeling of 'I' means identity which means identification. But even when you take 'I' out of the equation, the instinctive center and chief feature will still be there as a combination of physiological and psychological responses. They just won't congeal into identity. For instance, if you are naturally stubborn, you will still be resistant but it will be much less insistent and selfish and negative. If you are naturally dominant, it may still manifest as authority, but without being so overbearing and judgmental and heartless. If you are naturally fearful, fear will not overwhelm your entire being and make you obsessive or paranoid. And so on.

Is it true to say that transformation is the height of creation?

I know what you are saying, and yes. At the same time though, transformation is actually the opposite of creation which is a manifestation and proliferation of ethereal substance into lower and lower dimensions of matter and form. Conscious transformation moves in the other direction. It is an ascent of matter from form back to its divine source. This is the hidden majesty of transforming negative emotions and suffering. And the human being is a special form that makes this possible.

You once said that death marks the point where a third conscious shock is needed. Can you comment?

Death represents a release of energy from the human organism, which includes the free release of consciousness that had been housed in and tethered to the organism during its life. The question is how self-realized that energy is when death happens. The conscious shock at that point would be a much more comprehensive and all-inclusive realization of conscious awareness that is fully established as itself in an even higher dimension of itself. To be clear though, the fourth way does not mention a third conscious shock, although it is true that negative emotions represent one threshold, true suffering another, and death another. And there are likely further thresholds beyond the disappearance of the physical body.

And this transformation begins with not expressing negative emotions?

In the fourth way system, yes. Not expressing a negative emotion *for the purpose of awakening* changes the chemistry of the negative emotion. By containing its expression you gain control over the *physical* energy driving it. Its material starts to undergo a certain change. But you may still be identified with it internally because the energy is still tied up in your *psychological* sense of identity. Then you go a step farther and learn how not to identify on the inside, which not only separates the feeling if 'I' from the energy behind it, but makes possible a deeper recognition of the awareness that is seeing 'I'. The internal chemical process is now in full swing. Serious change can happen. A far more significant transmutation can take place to the point where you are no longer transforming just the negative emotion, but the sense if 'I' behind it, and most importantly the energy deep within it which can fuel and transform awareness itself. Very people are thinking about this and trying to swim in these waters. Instead they are venting negativity whenever the urge arises to do so.

Is it possible to transform a negative emotion after it has been expressed?

No, because when you express a negative emotion, two things happen: the energy gets converted—lowered—from psychological form into physical form; and in doing so it gets lost. It is now gone.

The idea behind non-expression and transformation is to *heighten* this energy inwardly. Not by suppressing or repressing it, but by purposely containing it so it can be distilled into a higher form. This is the esoteric meaning of alchemy.

Is it correct to say that even transformation produces some kind of waste matter and that the ego is this waste matter?

This would be true if the ego was a real thing, a real substance. But it is just an image projected in the mind, so there is nothing to be discharged. What might be considered the waste matter of transformation are the perceptions that filter from conscious awareness down to the mind where they take the form of teaching, writing, creativity in the arts, healing, human kindness, and compassion. In this sense you can think of waste matter as the byproducts of transformation.

Why is my energy so heavy sometimes? Like a physical weight?

That is the energy of the instinctive center. It is heavy because it is in fact a physical weight. It exists in physical form and operates with physical energy. Thoughts and emotions, on the other hand, are psychological. They exist in psychological form and operate with psychological energy which is faster, more volatile. This is why your thoughts can 'race' and your emotions can 'run away' with themselves. You feel heavy in your body. You feel upset in your mind. When you feel this heaviness, try to see it for what it is. Notice the entire body. Feel its energy as much as you can. Try to see how this heavy energy in the instinctive center wants to infiltrate and corrupt energy in the emotional and intellectual centers. See if you can find a way to keep it isolated to the instinctive center without showing it. As you do, try not to take it or yourself too seriously.

Why do athletes seem to perform better after getting mad and expressing negative emotions? Isn't that some kind of transformation?

It is a kind of transformation, but it is a *downward* conversion of energy. What usually happens is that the athlete is identified and consequently the energy in their four centers is all mixed up and interfering with each other, which affects their performance and makes them negative. Then they express the negativity. As this happens, they appear to have more energy because the surge of negativity has vitalized their ego as a *visible* identity. At the same time, the release of negative energy temporarily clears out the toxic mix of energy in their centers and they start to perform better—sometimes. Other times they implode and play even worse. It is a matter of circumstances and luck. Meanwhile, however, they have lost an extreme amount of psychic energy that can *never* be retrieved as material for conscious awareness.

If I am angry and I transform my anger, what happens to it?

If transformation actually occurs, the energy behind the anger is released to and resolves as the consciousness of awareness. The form it had taken as anger unforms and its original energy rejoins the field of consciousness. But this does not happen to your feeling of 'I'. That feeling is neutralized as soon as it is seen as just an image in the mind. Anger is just a psychological form the ego takes as a result of negatively charged energy, negative imagination, and identification all congealing into what we experience as anger. The same thing happens with all negative emotions. That is how they form. Without identification they cannot form. If they are already formed and you extract the identification, they fall apart and release their energy back to consciousness. This is why work on negative emotions forms the backbone of the fourth way. What you are doing is dismembering the sense of identity behind negative emotions and transcending it as conscious awareness.

Why do you think Gurdjieff made transformation sound like a trick without explaining it further?

He did not try to make it seem like a trick. The fact is that it is not easily described until you understand many other things that contribute to it. Even then it remains beyond words, beyond description. What Gurdjieff did say in a somewhat veiled way is that transforming negative emotions involves a 'special influence' over the emotions. He was referring to conscious awareness which is not something the mind can produce by effort. This 'special influence' stems from the realization that the notion of 'I' who feels negative is an illusory identity, and 'special influence' means consciousness looking behind the negative emotion and realizing that the feeling of 'I' behind it is just an image projected inside the mind. This seeing and this realization is a 'special influence' because it is emanating from a higher dimension of consciousness. That is another reason why Gurdjieff probably did not elaborate on it because transformation cannot happen in the second state of consciousness. It is a property or capacity that begins in the third state and carries over to the fourth state.

What corrupts negative emotions?

Negative emotions are themselves a form of corruption brought about by the wrong mixing of energy in different centers which we identify with as feelings of negativity. Identification enables the energy of one center to leak into other centers and foul them up. It is like diesel spilling into your gas tank and then both of them spilling into the radiator. Everything gets corrupted and the engine stops working, which is what happens to our emotional centers when we are negative. We stop perceiving reality and start pushing it away.

And yet you say that the energy of negative emotions is legitimate...

The energy behind negative emotions is legitimate in the sense that it is pure energy derived from the perceptiveness of consciousness. The impurity happens when this energy gets appropriated as a mental distortion that then gets solidified as an image of 'I'. "I am negative" is about as far away from pure consciousness as you can get in *psychological* form. And you get even farther away when the negativity gets expressed as *physical* energy.

Why is the instinctive center the engine of negative emotions?

The instinctive center is not the engine. It is the generator of the raw material for negative emotions. The engine is identification. The connection is that negative emotions form on the basis of separation, which is how the instinctive center views and reacts to the world. This sense of physical separation gets dramatically enhanced by the psychological feeling of 'I' that is brought on by identification: 'I' am separate from everyone and everything, and 'I' am negative about things *in relationship to* them. There is always some opposition or division or competition or 'enemy'. All that drops away with transformation. In its place comes an awareness of the whole. Even the seemingly worst, must unjust, most horrendous things are realized as having their place within the whole of creation and the purposes of life on earth. It doesn't mean you like them. It means you see them exactly as they are and as they are meant to be in this dimension as it relates to other dimensions of creation. Negative emotions evade this truth with distorted forms of rejection and interpretation and pushback.

The fourth way formulas for dealing with negative emotions sound nice, but all that changes when there is intense pain and depression.

Severe pain, turbulent thoughts, dark moods, and extreme energies are all aspects of the mind and body. They reside in the physiological and psychological realms, and consciousness can learn not to identify with them; not to be fooled into believing it is them. And, yes, that is hard until you start to see through the pain and depression. As you go deeper, you will see that *anything* you can perceive and feel in these realms is *never* the source which perceives them. You gain in strength to the extent that you understand this in the core of your being. This understanding opens the door to profound transformation. And it is true in relation to *everything* visible and invisible that consciousness can perceive in creation.

But the emotional pain is still there…

Each negative emption contains a degree of physical energy that stems from a negative reaction in the instinctive center. This negative energy rises in defense of something, and it helps when you can see what that something is because the negative energy behind it gets injected—by means of identification—into the emotional center where it takes shape as an attitude that furthers the ego's defense. The attitude is typically a justification for your feeling of blame or anger or resentment or self-pity. And behind all of them is your feeling of 'I' as a person who has been offended or hurt. So there is now a triple socket that includes the negative energy, the attitude, and the feeling of 'I'. Transformation occurs when consciousness unplugs itself from all three.

How do we unplug, as you say?

When you find yourself in the midst of suffering, consciousness can take either the 'down' escalator or the 'up' escalator. We can sink into the feeling of 'I' or rise as conscious awareness. We think we have to go along with the feeling of 'I', but that's not true. The mind and the body can suffer—and they are meant to suffer—but we as consciousness can choose to surround the suffering *as it passes through* the mind and body.

Does it help to give up my judgments?

It is not enough simply to drop the judgments and criticisms and blame that we impose on others. It is necessary to see through them to the source in ourselves from where the *urge* and the *need* to blame other people comes from. This is a closer examination of the ego. It is our identification with this core sense of self that we need to drop because the reality is that we judge and belittle and blame other people based on the expectations and requirements we have of ourselves *as an imagined identity*. It is this psychological cage that we have imprisoned awareness in, and in which we want to ensnare other people's ego. This is the norm for most of humanity and the cause for almost all the conflicts between people and nations. Even when people propose to give up their judgment they never can because they cannot give up their ego. It is just the ego proposing the idea of giving up judgment, and so the cycle continues.

Is the principle behind not expressing negative emotions to deny the ego?

Yes, although you have to understand that you are denying an illusion, a mental image. The principle is not to give this image any oxygen, not to vitalize it by indulging in and venting the energy behind it. When you contain this expression, you suffocate the ego and the material of its oxygen instead fills the sails of awareness. This is transformation. But you have to understand this method in all its detail and meaning. You have to see how it is about getting to the energy at *the source*. The form the negative emotion takes is secondary.

You said that transformation is unpleasant. Can you say more?

Transformation itself is pure, yet the process leading to it can seem nasty because all the toxins of identity need to be uprooted, purged, cleared out. This includes energy in the instinctive, emotional, and intellectual centers, all of which has been corrupted when it got distorted into a sense of identity. But to be clear, the unpleasantness is felt in the mind and body, not in consciousness, because it is in the mind and the body that the pressure of negativity and suffering is being contained before being transformed. Once that energy is transformed, the mind and body feel very light.

You also said negativity can serve as a reminder…

I meant in the sense that negative energy can become a signal that consciousness has fallen, or is falling, asleep in the feeling of 'I'. As a signal, it can thrust you out of 'I' into more conscious awareness.

Is the unpleasantness you described mainly in the instinctive center?

Mainly, yes. The instinctive center is never not involved in the creation, expression, and repression of negative emotions. It is always behind 'me' in some form. If there were no instinctive center there would be no raw material for negative emotions. If you look closely you will see that the emotional center never becomes negative by itself. To do so, it has to appropriate energy from the negative half of the instinctive center. You can see this in yourself and you can see it between couples where one person's instinctive center will pass negative energy to the other person's emotional center and then the other person will use that energy to become negative toward the first person. That is how fast and transferable this energy is. You see the same thing when one person is able to infuse and ignite negative passion in an entire crowd.

That seems to explain why we are most negative with those who are most dear to us.

It is strange how we can hurt those closest to us, and even stranger that we do it out of self-protection. The ego is determined to protect itself at all costs, and sometimes that cost is the loss of a relationship or friendship. But it also shows you how the ego is *designed* to create conflict in humanity. It is a strange design, but one with a purpose. Or, better yet, with a dual purpose because the ego is designed to be a vehicle for the expression of negative emotions as well as a catalyst for conscious self-realization.

Blame also seems to be a big part of relationships.

Blaming others for causing our negative emotions is very common. We even blame a bump on the sidewalk for making us trip. We turn around and snarl at it. It is the same thing. It is an attempt to externalize the source when in reality the source lies in ourself, in our ego, and in its foundation in the instinctive center. It demonstrates how peculiar the workings of the ego are and how bizarre the drama of human life on earth is.

What is really behind the itch to express negative emotions?

We are so accustomed to negative emotions that we think we should give way to them; that we are obliged to collapse into them and to *become* them. Doing so satisfies an itch, as you put in, in our imaginary picture of ourself. We want to be right, we want to set things straight, we want to punish people and circumstances for *seemingly* making us negative. When we scratch this itch, 'I' feels legitimate.

And can you talk a little more about how not identifying with them helps? What it does exactly?

By lessening identification, you open the space between the energy of the negative emotion, the psychological component that has coupled with that energy, and the awareness of seeing both. If you could follow a negative emotion in slow motion as it develops, you would see negatively-charged energy arising as a sensation in the instinctive center, then spilling into the emotional center and tainting it with negative feelings that get appropriated as a sense of 'me' that is further justified in the intellectual center. When you express the negative emotion, you legitimize the feeling of 'I'. But when you contain it and retrace it, you see that 'I' doesn't have to enter into the equation *if you don't identity* with the sensation and its companion emotion.

But the original sensation is still instinctive?

Yes. Negative emotions are a form of psychological *negation* that stems from instinctive *resistance*. The body reacts to something with a sensation of resistance and the mind backs it up with denial, rejection, opposition, negation. The original energy comes from the body's resistance, no matter how entangled the psychological negation becomes. This is why neither medication nor psychotherapy, nor the two together, can ever transform negative emotions. At best they can temporarily change the conditions *in* the mind and in the body, whereas transcendence occurs *beyond* the mind and body.

I have listened to you talk about negative emotions and I have read your book about transforming negative emotions, and I want to transform my negative emotions, but I keep finding myself up against a wall. Somehow I can't break through this wall.

All negative emotions are rooted in the notion of 'I' as a person. This is true of negative emotions that originate as a negative sensation in the instinctive center as well as what I call 'human' emotions which come as a result of deep personal loss, grief, and bewilderment. Consciousness itself is only disturbed by these physiological and psychological forms when it identifies with them and believes them as 'I' rather than seeing them as different forms of energy circulating within your being. Behind your question there is still the sense of 'I' and the belief in 'my' negative emotions. Maybe you can think of it another way. Envision, for instance, that you have been walking down a spiritual road and you come across a boulder blocking the road. The boulder, which is just an 'I', is trying to hinder your progress and persuade you to take a side road called defeat. And it is true that 'I' cannot go any farther. Consciousness itself has to find a way to climb over or walk around or somehow walk right through the boulder. I encourage you not to stop at this boulder and not to be afraid of it or dismayed by it. Pass through. Pass through. Be the consciousness and move on. And realize that this is only possible when you relinquish identification with the feeling of 'I'.

How will we know when we have transformed a negative emotion?

Negative emotions are noisy and dark. Transformation is silent and light.

~ ~ ~

The Silent Self

Echoes of the Mind

The Self is one.
Unmoving, it moves faster than the mind.

The Upanishads

THE MIND has been studied and talked about for millennia, yet it remains a mystery as to what it is, where it is, why it operates the way it does, and how it produces what we call thoughts and emotions. But the most overlooked factor in all this is that even though we cannot fully understand the mind, we can perceive it at work. Awareness can traverse the mind's caverns, valleys, and peaks. When you realize the significance of this, the mind and its contents become less important. Your concern turns increasingly to the matter of transcendence. Instead of surfing wave after wave in the hope of finally understanding your mind and identity, you lift into the air as pure presence.

How can I keep my mind from racing with thoughts?

There is a tiny switch that enables you to keep attention in the present, focused on what is right here in front of you, whatever you are doing. No one can flip this switch for you. You have to find it for yourself and, above all, you have to *want* to flip it. It is not a struggle against thoughts in the arena of the mind. It is a focus of awareness. You can think of it as a perch on a rock in the middle of a torrential river. Instead of trying to calm the waters of your mind, find this perch in yourself and try to get accustomed to the view from there.

Are you referring to the metaphysical realm?

You could say that, but we have to be clear about what you mean because there is a meta-physical and a meta-psychological realm, and a realm beyond both, and a realm beyond that. The way to keep it practical is to hold to the realization that you can notice the mind racing with thoughts *and* notice that you are noticing that. Then you gently hold onto that awareness and keep it focused.

Does that also apply to the problems in my life?

All problems are in the mind. They are just mental configurations, nothing more. These configurations are attached to the sense of 'I' being projected in the mind, and they usually take on the flavor of our chief feature. In reality they are just clouds in the mind. Pressure still exists in your life, but problems are all imaginary. Try to see the difference. If you take 'I' out of the equation, what happens to the problem? When you are not identified with a problem, how does it change? Try to spend a day facing all the problems in your life without seeing them as problems.

I feel like a stranger on earth. Do you feel that way?

It is not that we are strangers here, but that everything else—all appearances of form—are foreign to the source of consciousness that is behind our awareness of them. Consciousness recognizes, even without knowing itself, that none of these forms are real, and this produces a feeling of strangeness in the mind. This feeling can also become a sort of cue for consciousness to realize itself more fully.

How can we touch pure being?

We cannot. The best the mind can do is generate a thought about it and try to hold that. Only pure being can know itself and be itself.

The sense of 'me' and 'my' life feels so real. How can I see through this?

Behind all of our thoughts and feelings there is an ingrained belief about our life, its past, its future, and our sense as a person in relation to this reel of film. But it is all a series of images springing from the central pivot of 'I'. These images in turn generate thoughts and emotions that keep the notion of being a person in tact. When you peel them away, you come to the psychological foundation of 'I' which awareness is identified with and believes itself to be. If you manage to look underneath this foundation, there is no identity. There is just being, which is what you are at your deepest core. But consciousness usually passes through the human form without being aware of itself as consciousness.

And when this awareness does appear?

One reason this mystery of awareness goes unnoticed is that everything appears in awareness but awareness itself never appears. It simply perceives. This source of perception is always here behind the mind, but in most cases it is not conscious of being here. When it realizes itself being here, it does not appear as such. It simply comes into focus as itself.

Why is such a simple realization, as you describe it, so hard to reach?

Because consciousness is entrenched in multiple dimensions of its manifested forms. First you see your thoughts. Then you see the hologrammatic nature of thoughts. Then you see the projection of being a person having thoughts. Then you see the mental image of 'I' behind the person. Consciousness keeps realizing what it is *not* until it realizes the reality of itself. The same thing happens in relation to seeing the universe. Behind the manifestation of all its forms and dimensions there is something that is seeing all of them which can realize itself seeing them.

And yet the mind seems to bring us to this realization...

The mind itself is not conscious of existence. The moments of perception that we have about our existence stem from consciousness and these perceptions get reflected in the mind as thoughts *about* our existence. First consciousness, then the realization of existence, then thoughts about existence. From there we assume we can deepen our realization of existence by thinking about it more, but that is not true. The only way we can deepen it is by being more aware—simply knowing that we are being here with presence, not with thought. The mind can support us in this, but conscious awareness grows only from itself.

I find it useful to envision awareness as the neutral screen in the background.

In my experience this analogy can be extended further where the screen can be seen as the structure of the mind onto which the images of thoughts and feelings are being cast. This structure is indeed neutral, but it is not awareness. Awareness watches the film—the images of thoughts and emotions and 'I'—as they are cast onto the screen of the mind, and realizes itself as the light in the projector. Without this light, the rest cannot happen.

How do you account for so much beauty on the earth?

This is interesting because no single human is capable of perceiving and absorbing all the beauty and all the mystery behind the beauty. Is it possible that it exists—in its myriad details *and* as a whole—as an impression for another dimension of awareness? This seems likely to me.

Can you talk about conscience according to the fourth way?

Conscience is a reflection of wider consciousness that reverberates in and is felt by more or less the entire emotional center at once. It is like a light shown into all the nooks and crannies where 'I' resides. They are all exposed in a flash at the same time, which is why it is disconcerting to feel the pangs of conscience. Normally different groups of 'I's, and particularly different feelings of our sense of 'I', do not see each other and do not come into contact with one another. When they do it is a shock. But it is necessary from the perspective of consciousness so that consciousness can realize itself above all the 'I's and above our deepest sense of 'me' the person.

Why isn't awareness more obvious as our reality?

Because it is invisible, and because the perceptions made by awareness are immediately reflected in the mind where they create the feeling of 'I' perceived this and this is 'my' conclusion about it. The emphasis remains on 'me' and 'my' relationship to what 'I' have perceived. The truth about consciousness behind the original perception goes unrecognized and unrealized.

Can therapy help with identification?

It may help to a degree, although you have to understand that psychotherapy in general emphasizes problems without recognizing that their source is the notion of 'I' behind being a person who has problems. Identification runs deeper than you suspect. It's not as though there is identification and that you as the person get identified. It's that your sense of being a person is also a result of identification. Consciousness is identified with 'I' and 'I' is identified with its problems. But therapists don't regard identification as something that happens to consciousness. They attribute it to the ego and then try to resolve conflicts in the ego and in the ego's relationship to people and things. Meanwhile the underlying identification with 'I' remains.

But aren't some worries and fears legitimate?

The simple truth is that from the perspective of pure being there is nothing to be afraid of or to worry about. All of it is mind activity, mental turmoil. Pure being is no mind. The ultimate goal, if it can be called that, is to be entirely free of 'me', to leave 'I' behind, to see it drift away. The mind can't comprehend what this really means.

I get confused about who or what is trying to self-remember.

This is partly because self-remembering has degrees. It can be physical. It can be psychological. It can be metaphysical. In the body and mind it is experienced as a concentration of attention in one or more of the four centers. In consciousness it is purely a realization of awareness. It might help, when you are trying to self-remember, to notice that you are trying to do it. Be aware of that, too. There is another degree of self-remembering that comes as you release identification with the *effort* to self-remember.

Ouspensky spoke in his lectures about different kinds of influences that govern our life. Do you consider this a major idea in the system?

He was referring to influences which are always acting on humanity, such as wars, religions, scientific discoveries, big inventions, and social upheavals. This includes emanations from the galaxy, the sun, the planets, the earth, and the moon. And we can now include the thousands of satellites circling the earth which tie into an extensive infrastructure of electronic towers, continental cables, computers, and smartphones all over the earth. When you hold a smartphone you are serving as a conductor for this infrastructure. You are both a psychological transmitter and a physical 'ground' for the electronic flow of energy. This is not a small thing. It is a big change on the scale of humanity, and it is affecting individual lives in many ways both psychologically and physically. In particular it is providing a new kind of conduit for identification and conflict.

Ouspensky was trying to explain the significance of how these influences—the man-made ones—

have continually increased throughout history in a way that has rendered mankind more mechanical and more dependent on mechanical influences as opposed to conscious influences. This whole idea is not a major tenet of the fourth way, but it is significant. As Ouspensky said, at a certain point in the study of ourselves it is important to look outside ourselves and see the world around us through the larger lens of the system.

Do you consider the psychology and the cosmology of the fourth way as two separate systems?

I see them as different sides of the same glove. Turn each one inside out and you have the other. They also mirror and reflect each other. By understanding one you gain insight into the other and vice versa. I also see them as a figure eight where the two circles touch at a single point. In the top circle are all the system ideas about cosmology, which is the world of the universe. In the lower circle are all the system ideas about psychology, which is the inner world of man. The single point where they conjoin is what the fourth way calls essence. Without this, the two realms don't connect and feed into one another. The point of essence also conveys the significance of being in this human form which is a gateway between dimensions.

A gateway to what?

A gateway for the seed of consciousness to pass either up or down in the ray of creation. Essence is a seedcase of consciousness. You could say that essence is the human side of consciousness as well as the conscious side of being human. It is simple presence. The more it identifies, the more human it becomes. The more it remembers itself, the more conscious it becomes. The same thing is true of the absolute pure being at the source of all creation. We stand on a similar threshold on a different scale, but the transformation that is possible on this threshold is the same, which is the meaning of man being made in god's image. It is very unique to find ourselves here in human form. It is very special, very sacred.

How do you describe the difference between the mind and identity?

The mind is an amazing device because it converts the reflections of awareness into psychological form. We take this so much for granted that we never actually examine how it works. Thoughts, emotions, concepts, words, labels, and opinions are all forms that take shape in the mind as a result of the reflections of perception. Perception gives rise to reflections and reflections give rise to these psychological forms. When the consciousness behind perception identifies with these forms, it attaches to and forms around them as the ego, or what the fourth way calls imaginary 'I'. The mind can exist without this identity, but our sense of identity cannot exist without the mind.

Why do you single out judgment as such a big thing?

Rather than recognize and honor the light of consciousness in each other, we judge, condemn, criticize, and belittle each other's *form of identity*. Our imaginary feeling of 'I' judges what we perceive as the imaginary 'I' of other people, and this underlies the psychology of human relationships, cultural misunderstandings, and global conflicts. It is a big thing in that it is a delusion which everyone considers to be normal. We think our judgments are rational, justified, and correct. Meanwhile it is all a distortion stemming from the ego.

In other words, judgment is a kind of false labeling?

Yes, and it includes more than just human relationships. For instance, take away all the labels that we call 'names'. Take away the label of 'human being'. Take away the labels of 'race' and 'color' and 'gender' and 'culture'. Take away the labels of 'nature' and 'creation'. Without the labels, what are all these phenomena? More importantly, what is behind them and beyond them? And how do they all tie together? There is a reality manifesting in us and all around us and we fail to see it because we are identified with forms and names and concepts. And then we judge our interpretation of these concepts.

Identity also seems like a box with a label.

And it is interesting to think about what is inside the box. For instance, envision putting light in a bunch of boxes that seem to give the light visible form. Then assign different names to each box and forget about the light inside, which is akin to putting a lock on each box. Then condemn or praise the form of each box which is like throwing away the key.

What are the sciences missing in their exploration of awareness?

Philosophers, psychologists, and scientists don't realize that the mind cannot stand outside consciousness and study consciousness. Only consciousness can do that. For the mind, consciousness can be only a concept. Consciousness is more than that, but it cannot be seen or measured by the mind. It can seem as though we are talking in a circle when describing this, but it becomes clear once you step out of the circle. Surprisingly, this step is always very close. Right now, for instance, we can be conscious of the fact that we are talking. Or more accurately, there is something—an awareness—that can be conscious of the fact that we are talking. This awareness can simultaneously see us talking and realize that it is seeing us. In other words, it can be conscious of itself as awareness, or aware of itself as consciousness. This is not normally the case with most people most of the time, but the potential is always right here. And this potential lies at the heart of what the fourth way calls self-observation and self-remembering.

Do you believe in premonitions?

Premonitions and déjà vu may be memories of the future. Remember that the future used to be the past and the past was at one point the future. Time is not what we think. Neither are premonitions. But this truth is dangerous when it gets into the hands of the four centers.

How so?

Because imagination is so compelling in us, in the mind. You have to be able to separate out the clouds of imagination and see with piercing clarity, and only conscious awareness can do that. And then you see that even a premonition is just a reflection, a hint, cast into the mind.

Is identification a force, like an electric current?

That is what it feels like in extreme form, but it can also be very subtle. Identification is the unconscious momentum of consciousness as it projects itself into dimensions of form. The rest of what we usually call identification is the *result* of identification—the effect it is has on the four centers which operate differently under the influence of identification. They become more frenetic, more compulsive, impatient, insistent, and so on. Identification causes us to take ourselves as a person more seriously. As this happens, it prompts our urge to be negative and to express negativity.

What is happening to awareness in the three states?

When we are in the second or waking state, awareness is attached to the mind and body as it walks, talks, forms opinions, makes decision, and performs actions. When we dream in the top of the first state, it is attached mainly to the mind. When we are in deep sleep at the bottom of the first state, it rests in itself, although it is not conscious of resting as itself. In the third state, awareness is conscious of itself. These are all degrees of the same consciousness.

What is the spiritual void?

It is the infinite field of consciousness which is conscious of itself and of everything within it.

That sounds pretty vague.

Consider how everything might appear to you if there was no physical body filtering everything with its senses, and no mind interpreting everything as concepts and labels. And without a sense of identity standing between you and reality. Just reality and the pure perception of reality, and pure consciousness in and behind that pure perception.

But how to actualize that?

Yes, that is the whole point. It always starts with being conscious of being here right now and being conscious of the fact that you are conscious right now, and realizing that you are not this person but the consciousness of this person. The rest you discover on your own. More accurately, consciousness discovers the rest on its own. It is not about us as a person. It is all about consciousness.

What is the best way to make that leap?

Open up. Let go of the urge to grasp, pin down, understand, and resolve everything. Resort simply to awareness and allow it to realize itself as it perceives. Hold to this more and more and more. Trust that the rest will reveal itself and the truth about itself. Don't be afraid of what feels like the insecurity of letting everything play second fiddle to conscious awareness. It doesn't mean you stop living the life of a human being. It means you become more and more conscious as the witnessing presence that is less and less and less attached to the identity and life it is witnessing.

Is there a way to recognize the astral body?

Gurdjieff said higher bodies form inside lower ones; that conscious awareness takes shape as the astral body inside the four centers where it is bound until it fully coagulates and crystallizes, at which point it can expand beyond the four centers and become capable of independent existence after the death of the body. This is the theory. You have to examine it from your own experience. The question is, can you recognize this in yourself without fooling yourself about it? Gurdjieff also pointed out that no one is born with an astral body. Although everyone is born as a *conduit* for awareness, that does not mean awareness will automatically recognize itself and coagulate as the self-realization of pure being. It has to become conscious of its own being as consciousness. This is what all spiritual teachings throughout all time have pointed to.

How does it coagulate, as you say?

Conscious awareness becomes more and more familiar with the beingness of itself. As it does, this self-realization deepens to a point where it has itself fully in focus. The mind envisions this as becoming more solid, more of an entity, but that it not the case. It simply means consciousness being fully conscious as consciousness. But even that is not the end. The word fully implies much more than 'done'.

Is the fourth way being lost?

Theoretically, the fourth way appears and disappears in relation to the socio-political climate of cultures. My assumption is that it will not be lost until humanity is entirely lost. At the same time it has been somewhat obscured in the twenty-first century by non-duality teachings, Zen, Buddhism, the popularization of mindfulness, and the commonly accepted notion that everyone can wake up.

Does chief feature become the ego?

Not exactly. The ego is like insulating wire around chief feature. It helps ensure the conductivity of identification. Without the ego encapsulating chief feature, the lightning force of identification cannot 'strike' with sufficient energy. The reverse happens as chief feature diminishes and normalizes, so to speak. It provides less conductivity for identification.

Is the direct path the easiest?

Not necessarily the easiest. It is more accurate to say that it *can be* the most *direct*. But that does not make it easy because the mind is both clever and naïve. It thinks it can travel the direct path whereas the direct path is for consciousness only. The indirect or progressive path, on the other hand, includes the mind because it is designed to show a receptive mind the full extent of what awareness is *not*, and by doing so bring the mind to its limit where it faces the chasm of consciousness. But the mind never enters that chasm. You have to be either well prepared or deeply intuitive to recognize this distinction. Another way to say it is that the direct path begins with self-remembering whereas the progressive path begins with self-observation. In right order they lead to the same thing and contain elements of each other.

Does chief feature develop as a dependency on others?

You could say that, but it depends on what is behind your question.

I was thinking that different people impose different kinds of requirements on other people, but that all requirements indicate a sort of dependency.

In general, yes. People with passive chief features tend to have an identity that is rooted in needing reassurance and affirmation from others and from circumstances, whereas people with active chief features tend to have an identity rooted in needing to control others and to control their circumstances. In both cases, the sense of identity does not get very far without the relationship to other people.

Is sleep the prison or are they two different things?

They are different analogies for the same thing. Spiritual 'sleep' is often described as the four centers holding awareness prisoner, but that's not quite correct. What is holding awareness prisoner is its identification with the four centers. It's really holding itself prisoner as a feeling of identity in the centers. Escaping means waking up to and transcending this attachment to identity, which is what identification is.

The more I see identification in myself, the more I feel lost in its maze. What's the best thing to do at that point?

You have to work your way backwards through identification until you reach the point where it begins. It is very interesting when you discover the threshold of it in yourself; the exact point where non-identification starts to become identification. It is the same point where consciousness starts to become conscious of being conscious. *Everything hinges on that point.* So keep seeing identification without identifying with seeing it. Move past that and keep feeling your way to a place of non-identification. This place is deep inside your being. It is not indifference or passivity. It is simply *being* without anything attached to it.

When I catch myself rejecting things in my life I try to accept them and that works for awhile, but it doesn't last and I find myself back in rejection mode.

This is because acceptance and rejection are both postures of the mind. It is the same gate swinging either open or closed. Non-identification is something else. It is not the mind. It is a clear state of consciousness. Acceptance can help promote it, but non-identification happens beyond acceptance, on the other side of the fence. So instead of trying to hold onto acceptance with the mind, try to use acceptance as a trampoline to bounce consciousness over the fence to where it belongs. This is the right use of the mind.

Can you talk about the obstacles to self-remembering?

All the obstacles to self-remembering stem from identification. Identification is a condition of consciousness having lost consciousness *as itself* and collapsed into whatever it is conscious *of*. Imagination, lying, unnecessary talk, inner-considering, and negative emotions are all a result of identification. They are variations on the theme of identification. They cannot happen without identification. And although they seem like obstacles that consciousness has to overcome, they are really conditions of consciousness itself which in turn have an effect on the lower centers. So the goal is not to try to change the effect in the centers. The goal is for consciousness to bring *itself* back into focus. When that happens, the effects start to diminish.

And yet it is right to struggle against the effects, yes?

Yes, in the sense of struggling against identification. For instance, if you catch yourself daydreaming, you want to pull awareness out of the stream of imagination and be conscious of where you are and what you are doing. This is different than trying to stop the stream. Trying to stop imagination itself is useful as an exercise, but what happens is that we end up struggling to stop the stream, which feels valid when in fact we are still identified. We fail to realize that the goal is for awareness just to get out. The same thing is true with inner-considering. Although it is useful to try to stop it when you feel it, the goal is not just to stop it; the goal is to use it as a reminder for awareness to get out; to pull itself out of that form of identification, that dimension of being asleep. The situation is somewhat different with negative emotions because they are the result of a confluence of identification, imagination, and inner-considering. To see the full implications of this, you have to stop their outward expression and shine the light of awareness back into the psychological realm where negative emotions took shape in the first place. You cannot do this successfully if you express the negative emotion because all the material behind it is then combusted and lost.

Is the world just a projection of the mind?

It is a projection *in* the mind as seen by the mind. But this is just a theory until it becomes a reality for you. In terms of us as human beings, it is not that trees, for example, don't exist. It is that we don't see them for what they really are because we are interpolating the appearance of their form through the mind and through the labels and concepts the mind imposes on trees. This is true of everything we perceive. There are invisible layers of dimensions behind all the visible forms we see. In what the fourth way calls the second state of consciousness, we see only the surface of things.

How can I increase my understanding?

What we call understanding is a psychological interpretation and organization of the reflections of perception which *follow perception*. These reflections form as thoughts about what we see. Instead of seeing, we see our thoughts about what we see. The more you focus on seeing, the more understanding will increase. This applies to anything you try to learn in depth, not just to spiritual growth.

I get the feeling that some teachers are talking way over my head.

Sometimes they are forced to because the questions they receive are not specific enough. For instance, some teachers who may reside on the twelve floor try to explain the view they see to people on the first floor. They describe how things look from 'above', but it is received as just mental concepts by those below. Those below then presume that they ought to be able to go right to the twelfth floor, when their questions are best directed as, "how can I get to the next floor or the next few floors above where I am now?"

An example would be the desire to transform negative emotions without understanding how negative emotions form, why containing them through non-expression is helpful, and what transformation really means. Does the twelfth floor really exist? Yes. Does that mean you can instantaneously realize yourself there? Yes. But very few people find that elevator. Most have to take the stairs. And it is fine to take the stairs. It doesn't matter how you get there.

Why do some have to take the stairs?

Most people need some degree of preparation and adjustment because their sense of identity is entrenched in the four centers. Things have to be shaken and loosened and released before the finest energy in them can find its way to transformation.

You mean it is too locked up in the ego?

Yes, you can think of it like that. The more you see the ego for what it is, the more you see it as just a mental projection; an image cast into the mind; and that the same thing is true of each thought and feeling that passes through the mind. Most people are living their lives from a sense of 'I' in this projection which means that all the dynamics of humanity are based on this. It is startling when you first see this. Then you adjust to the fact that it is supposed to be this way as part of the chemistry of organic life on earth.

And the ego is never happy for long…

Most people are unhappy in some way with their sense of themselves. Even those who intuit that their sense of self is artificial do not see all the way to the root of their dissatisfaction because they are inside the sense of 'I' rather than looking at 'I' from consciousness.

Can you give examples of the distinctions between the different levels of men according to the fourth way?

Men number 1-2-3 refers to people in whom consciousness is more or less congealed in the four centers of the mind and body as an entrenched sense of ego. Man number four refers to someone invested in spiritual evolution enough that consciousness has begun to loosen and be less entrenched in, but still under the influence of, the ego. Man number five refers to someone in whom consciousness has started to realize itself as consciousness such that it is gaining free circulation *within* the four centers but is still limited by them. Man number six refers to someone in whom consciousness is more independent of the centers, and man number seven even more so. The higher the level of conscious awareness, the more independent it is of the four centers.

How does this progression happen? Are their signposts?

When you can see yourself as a man number 1-2-3, you are on the verge of being a man number 4. When you can see your feeling of 'I' as a man number four *trying to* awaken, you are on the verge of being a man number 5, and so on. But, again, this is just a description. The seer I am referring to comes from conscious awareness, not from the mind. It resides beyond the mind, beyond the ego, beyond the seeing.

What do you mean by 'see yourself?'

It is like a painting with a foreground, middle ground, and background. The four centers are in the foreground. Your sense of 'I' is in the middle ground. Awareness is in the background. We are usually in the middle ground preoccupied with the foreground while the background, which is like the endless horizon, goes unnoticed to itself. The foreground and middle ground are limited, but the background is not. The only thing lacking is its consciousness of itself as the background against which the middle and fore grounds exist.

But that is just fourth way theory, right?

All ideas and teachings are intellectual scaffolding assembled in different ways around the void of awareness. The scaffolding is a mental apparatus, nothing more. Its benefit is that it provides a framework for consciousness to realize itself as the void *inside and outside us.* This void of *being* is invisible, yet it is more real than everything else. You have to come to the reality of it for yourself, but theories are meant to help. They are a support.

But then they become opinions…

They may sound opinionated, yes, but in that case they have lost their value. Opinions, attitudes, and judgments consolidate around our feeling of self. Meanwhile, conscious awareness transcends all of this: the entire mind, the entire feeling of 'I' in the mind, and all the mental and emotional activity swirling around in both. An opinion is a very little thing, but in sleep we don't see it this way. We consider ourselves clever to have opinions, and we cling to them.

Can you give a quick, short definition of awakening?

Awakening is the withdrawal of consciousness from its identification with 'I', brought about by the self-realization of seeing 'I' and simultaneously knowing itself as the seeing. This becomes the basis of conscious awakening.

What about the person?

When we manifest as the person, consciousness projects itself into the psychological and physical dimensions. In most instances, consciousness loses recognition of itself as consciousness, identifies with its projection, and becomes a sense of 'I' as the person. The spiritual meaning of ignorance is consciousness ignoring itself, losing realization of itself, forgetting itself. But this is not necessary. Consciousness can regain and retain recognition of its core presence while projecting itself as attention in the four centers of the mind and body. While manifesting as the person, it can also knowingly retain itself as consciousness.

Do you mean not identifying as 'I'

Yes. It is a matter of consciousness learning not to become the form it projects in the psychological world. It has to refrain from attaching itself to this form instead of stepping into it. It has to stay home in itself, as itself.

What about the feeling of being hurt?

You can be injured physically and offended psychologically, but consciousness cannot be touched by either. It is a different dimension.

But 'I' feel hurt.

'I' is in the psychological realm. It is the form that consciousness takes in that realm when it is identified. But the source—pure consciousness—is beyond that.

Is there a difference between the feeling of 'I' and the feeling of being present?

It depends on what you mean by the feeling of being present because presence itself is not a feeling or sensation. What usually happens is that presence appears and this creates a reaction in the mind and body. A common example is the mental formation of "I am present." But this is not the consciousness of awareness. It is the result of awareness. It is a reflection of awareness in the mind. Look closely and you will see that awareness is right there just behind that feeling of 'I'. It is what enables you to see 'I' forming as a thought or emotion.

It makes me wonder what identity really is…

The fact that we experience identity in human form is astonishing; just the fact that it exists as a feeling of identity, which is something that rocks and plants and animals and perhaps even planets don't experience. Also astonishing is how deceptive the feeling of identity is; that it is just a mental projection—nothing more. This magic show we are caught up in as the notion of being a person is very unusual.

And desire seems to play a big part in it.

As the ego, we keep waiting for 'something else' or the 'next thing' to happen. There is rarely a *complete* collapse into consciousness as consciousness because it gets displaced by the urge to do something or avoid something, and this momentum sustains the sense of 'I' which is the ego. This is also where you find desire and fear. Both of them form as bait that lures awareness into identification. The ego is certain that it needs something it does not have or that it needs to avoid what is happening or may happen. It is all a mental trap.

And when we avoid the trap?

The more consciously and deeply awareness resides in itself as consciousness, the more sacred it becomes. Sacred is also just a word for something that cannot be described in words, just as total freedom cannot be explained in words.

Do you mean transcending the mind?

Yes, although transcendence is not one thing. Consciousness continually steps out of and beyond multiple levels of form—physical, cellular, psychological, metaphysical—during its ascension and return to its source as pure being. This is why certain molecular moods, psychological visions, and even psychedelic experiences can be hard to transcend. They seem legitimate on their own level. It is incomprehensible to those forms and the identity experienced in them to realize that there is something more pure, more real, beyond all of them. Ultimately consciousness transcends *everything*. But this comes much later. The first step is to watch your thoughts and feelings in their psychological arena and realize that you can see them and be aware of seeing them. The next step is to notice the sense of 'I' attached to them and to realize that you can also see that while being aware of seeing it. You cannot move to higher levels of transcendence all at once. Yes, that is possible—which is what the direct path talks about—but it is rare. Even what may appear to be a direct jump is the inevitable result of an accumulation of experience and preparation.

Nevertheless, my thoughts and emotions feel real, especially when they are intense. The idea of just transcending them seems idealistic.

Instead of seeing thoughts and emotions as solid objects, see them as transparent liquid and dive right into them and through them, absorbing them as you go. Consciousness not only manifests everything out of itself, it transforms everything back into itself. This is the mystery of being and creation. What we are really after is conscious participation in this mystery. So don't be afraid of your thoughts and emotions, and don't fight them. Welcome them. Let them pass right through you unhindered. Allow them to resolve themselves in the core of your being as consciousness.

Sometimes I think everything would be just fine if I stopped insisting on my idea of the future.

We don't realize how imaginary the future is and how much we validate what is just a projection in our mind. This projection obscures consciousness, which gets entangled in it, and becomes a tension rod of anxiety that winds tighter and tighter the more we identify with it. But it is just imagination. It has nothing to do with the present right now.

And yet I feel compelled to plan for the future and as a result I worry about it.

If there was no intellectual center and no emotional center, we could not project a future. Animals don't project a future. Nor do plants. It is entirely a man-made, mind-made phenomenon. Our belief in it as also mind-made. This belief is so strong that whole industries have been built around it, and these industries exert great pressure on egos to worry about the future and invest in it and be afraid of *the idea* of the future. Meanwhile, consciousness itself never ventures there because the future is nothing more than a mental projection. Only the mind can go there in its dreams. Meanwhile, the mind, which has become an extension of the ego, is loathe to give up its notions about the future even though that notion creates considerable suffering.

But isn't it right for the mind to look after the body?

It sounds strange to say this, but the body and mind are not actually aware of each other or of themselves. The body does not perceive the mind at all. And what the mind thinks are its perceptions of the body are really interpretations in the mind that result from reflections of consciousness. The mind and body are dead to each other without consciousness. If anything, we could say that the body looks after the mind by looking after itself, which it does *automatically*, but that is not consciousness.

Are the mind and body both averse to pressure?

Yes. And in both instances, when pressure presents itself, you can choose not to turn away immediately, and to instead turn toward it gently and step through it gracefully. Why? Because what we call pressure can be a catalyst for deepening the self-realization of awareness. This is an important aspect of being human because we cannot by ourselves create the energy that pressure creates for us. At the same time, we have learned to dislike and avoid the force of pressure. It is useful to examine what this force really is and why it is so necessary for the transformation of consciousness.

Can you talk about active seeing?

I would call it aware seeing or conscious seeing. The word 'active' implies awareness going out and getting whatever you are looking at, whereas conscious awareness stays home and welcomes into itself what it perceives. Conscious awareness also does more than see things. It absorbs the energy embodied in what it sees. Everything psychological, physical, natural, and man-made embodies different qualities of energy and conscious awareness feeds off of their energy. This is another meaning of what transformation is.

How can we manifest love more often?

As the mind and body, we misunderstand what love is. Conscious awareness manifests *as* love and we feel its reflection in the emotional center, but that reflection and feeling are not love. Behind the word love is something deeper than even the deepest love we can feel. In answer to your question, I would say try to manifest awareness as consciously as you can without trying to exude a sense of love and without being concerned about being loving or appearing to be loving. Love comes. We don't create it.

How does consciousness feed off things it perceives?

An exchange takes place when we eat, when we breath, and when we perceive. Eating is the slowest and longest exchange. Breathing is faster and shorter. Perceiving directly from consciousness is immediate. In all three instances energy gets exchanged and transformed in different ways. This is the principle behind the idea of the food diagram in the fourth way. But you can see for yourself that looking at concrete has a different effect on you than looking at a mountain stream. You can discern the difference between traffic noise and Beethoven's Ninth Symphony.

The finer the energy, the more closely it resonates with consciousness. This does not make some impressions better than others. It just makes them more immediately digestible. In fact, there is a lot to digest if you are able to really see concrete for what it is, where it came from and why, what purpose it serves, and what its life span implies. Everything is material for conscious awareness.

Obviously that doesn't apply when we are identified with looking at something...

Yes, because then we don't see the reality and full truth about the object. We see only its outer form and surface, usually in terms of the label we have given it—such as 'concrete'. But just as there is a point of complete identification, there is a point of complete non-identification, and from there everything is seen more deeply. In the case of concrete, try to unpeel the label and look deeper into the life of what you are seeing. This is very useful as an intellectual exercise.

Why does the miracle of awareness seem so negligible at times?

Because that is how the mind thinks of it. Or, more accurately, it is because the mind cannot perceive awareness and therefore cannot properly think about it. When you learn about consciousness it seems to be on the same level, or in the same realm, as thoughts, emotions, and sensations. But gradually it dawns that consciousness encompasses all of them and can transcend all of them.

How does the moon make us negative?

The moon itself does not directly cause identification or negativity. What happens is that the gravitational force of its pull creates tension on the earth as well as in our human bodies and minds. The normal reaction to this tension is to identify with it and react with negative emotions which in turn feed the magnetic field of the moon in some way. So there is an exchange of energy between the moon and organic life on earth which includes humanity as its most sensitive instrument for reception and transmission of this energy. This is also an interesting question because it is not necessary to identify with the influence of the moon or to become negative when we feel its pressure. But for this consciousness has to be more aware and not get caught in the exchange.

~ ~ ~

The Silent Self

The Hologram of 'Me'

When the time comes,
you are awakened as if from a dream.

Pai-Chang

CONSCIOUSNESS is invisible and real whereas the 'I' of ego, which feels like a legitimate identity, is simply the projection of an image in the mind. The more you see this projection in yourself, the more it appears as a *notion* of self. What sees this, however, is not 'you' as the mind or ego, but consciousness itself which is not an 'I' or a 'you' or an entity with identity. Words can never describe the reality of this self-realization of consciousness.

How does 'I' disappear?

The image of 'I' unforms the same way it formed. The determining factor is identification. The more identified you are, the more real the image appears. The less identified you are, the less real it appears.

How does the mind project this image?

The human mind is based on a similar principle of design as the universe. Both are a structure in whose space objects move and turn and reflect light. Take away the terms 'universe' and 'mind' and you will see essentially the same phenomenon on different scales. Your question could also be, "How does the source of pure consciousness project what appears to be the universe?"

Sometimes enlightenment seems so simple. Then it seems profound. Then it seems ridiculous even.

Enlightenment, self-realization, and awakening, or whatever you choose to call it, is all of these things, depending on where it is being viewed from. To just the intellectual center it may seem far-fetched. To the emotional center it may seem profound. To consciousness itself it is very simple. This simplicity also becomes more and more profound.

In terms of 'I' as an image in the mind, where does that leave difficult past experiences?

The past also resides in the mind around the sense of 'I', 'me', 'my' life. Whatever the experience, it comes down to unlocking this sense of self behind the pain and seeing it as a mental image, a psychological hologram, and realizing that you are realizing that. When this happens there is less need to revisit or purge past experiences. Any genuine pain associated with experiences will surface as the light of consciousness shines brighter and wider and deeper. The energy behind experiences gets released and reabsorbed as consciousness. It has nothing to do with 'I'. 'I' was keeping the pain intact psychologically and physically. When 'I' is dissolved, the energy behind pain is unlocked and made available either for release or for transformation.

What about deep feelings of hurt that are legitimate?

They are legitimate in the sense that they happened and that they hurt. At the same time, what felt hurt was 'I'. So you have to go deeper than the hurt and see the feeling of 'I' behind it. Even if you resolve the hurt—for example through therapy—you will still be left with the sense of 'I' behind it. The source will not have been severed at its root. This is true with all negative emotions. They cannot form without the nucleus of 'I', and 'I' cannot take shape without identification. The whole thing is about identification, particularly identification with our feeling of 'I'. Remember, too, that nothing can ever touch or hurt consciousness itself because it is a different dimension of being.

So the mind has to keep finding its way to pure presence?

The mind can never find its way to pure presence because the mind is never more than an anticipation of or reaction to what unfolds in the present. The mind is never *here* when things unfold. It is too slow for that.

I asked you earlier if the direct path is the easiest. What about is it faster than the progressive path?

It is like whittling a stick. On the progressive path you whittle and whittle and whittle until you see through all that you are not. At that point the only thing left is consciousness and it realizes itself. Alternatively, you can intuit while whittling or even before whittling that it is going to end in nothing left, and you jump right to consciousness. What usually happens, however, is a combination of both. You whittle a little, then you intuit consciousness, but you cannot sustain the purity of consciousness because you continue to be identified with something in yourself—with some element of 'I' that has a hold over consciousness—and you have to go back to whittling some more to get at the root of it. In the end it is not a matter of easier or faster or better. It is a matter of full realization. Complete non-identification. Unadulterated consciousness.

So that's what you mean that the whole thing is about identification?

Yes, in the sense that identification is the stick we are whittling. Behind the term 'identification' is a universal law similar to gravity which compels consciousness to attach itself to and experience itself as the many forms that manifest out of the source of itself. It's as though the pure being at the source of consciousness is constantly manifesting forms and then using its consciousness to chase them. Isn't this odd? Even more odd is that the form of a human being provides the opportunity for consciousness to rediscover and realize itself and return to the source of itself by not attaching to forms. Most of creation is not designed this way. It seems to be unique to our experience as human beings that consciousness can realize itself in us and return to the source of itself.

You said therapy may not get at the real root of the problem. Is that right?

The question to be asked about psychotherapy is, where is it intended to bring you, and who is 'you'? Who is undergoing therapy and who hopes to benefit from it. The word therapy means to cure: what exactly is your therapy trying to cure? The better you understand this, the better the result. But this is a big topic that easily gets confused because you have to be clear about the distinction between the 'I' of ego and the consciousness of awareness. For instance, as you undergo therapy, can consciousness observe yourself undergoing it and can consciousness remain unidentified with the person it sees going through it? The problem is not the root of the problem, and the ego is not the root of the problem. The root is identification with the 'I' of ego. As I mentioned earlier, take away 'I' and see what happens to the problem.

Can't we ask the same thing about enlightenment? Where is enlightenment supposed to bring us?

Yes. This is a good question to ponder. What is enlightenment and where is it supposed to lead? What happens once you see the view from the mountain top, especially given that teaching and learning are primarily mental exercises designed to help you get to the top? But what then? What would it mean, for instance, for consciousness not only to behold the view but to leave the mind and body, take flight from the mountain top, and *be-*

come the view? What is that relative to the sense of identity you feel now? Can *that* know itself now? It is also a good question because no one can answer it for you.

It's meant to bring us to our true nature, isn't it?

Most of nature's life forms—mineral, plant, and animal—exist to survive and proliferate. This is their reason for existing in the form they do. Human beings also exist to survive and proliferate, but there is something more because humans include the seed of conscious awareness. This is a marked distinction, yet it goes mostly unnoticed and undiscovered.

And this is why we can become enlightened...

Yes, but you have to understand that you as the person don't become enlightened. The consciousness of awareness realizes itself above and beyond 'you'. As it self-realizes, the mind and body remain while the hologram of 'I' dissolves. The transformation of consciousness is wordless. It silently and invisibly 'knows' it is here. And this possibility is what distinguishes us from other forms of life.

But the desire to seek comes from the person?

Indirectly, yes. Seeking and striving for awakening is right for the mind, but consciousness does neither. It just *is*. Even trying to stop seeking is still an idea in the mind with its root in the ego. It is still 'me' wanting something and wanting to be something by trying not to be something. Consciousness is out of this loop.

Is it important to understand how the four elements of nature are working in us and through us?

The four elements are esoteric code for the four centers. Earth is the instinctive center. Water is the moving center. Air is the intellectual center. Fire is the emotional center. In the fourth way, the four elements also represent the idea of carbon, oxygen, and nitrogen combining in different ways to form variations of hydrogen. The idea is that all matter in the universe is made of the same substance in different degrees of density, speed of vibration, and combinations of triads.

Why is it so hard to abandon the ego?

It seems hard to the mind because the ego is entrenched in the mind. It is the ego trying to abandon its idea of the ego. In actuality there is nothing to abandon and nothing to abandon it. This becomes clear when consciousness self-realizes and pierces the illusion of the ego as an identity. The hologram of 'I' goes 'poof' and you are left with just the pure being of consciousness.

How can I see my center of gravity?

Each center of gravity is a filter for how perceptions get formulated *in* the mind, and a conduit for how those formulations get expressed *by* the mind. Intellectually centered people are prosaic. Emotionally centered people are poetic. Moving centered people are pragmatic. Instinctively centered people are tactile. These are just generalizations to give you an idea of the differences and how you can discern the differences. If it is not clear to you, don't worry about it. Keep observing as impartially as you can and it will reveal itself.

Does my center of gravity affect how I think about awakening?

Yes. Each center of gravity generates its own concept of what awakening might mean. For some people it is more about the mind. For some it is an emotional feeling. For others it is about the body. Intellectually centered people want to solve the knowledge puzzle of awakening. Emotionally centered people want awakening to resolve their dilemmas. Instinctively centered people are more interested in heightening their energy. And so on. This is why it can be helpful to know about center of gravity. It gives you a clearer contrast in yourself about what consciousness *is not*.

Do changes happen in a person who awakens?

Changes may happen to the person, but they are not a true mark of anything. The real mark, which is not a mark, is the self-realization of consciousness and the pure being at its source. Everything else is just a side effect in the mind and body.

What is the connection between chief feature and the ego?

The spinal cord of the instinctive center and the sheath of chief feature entwined around it form the superstructure of the ego. In this conglomeration there are points where the instinctive center and chief feature are directly joined, and these become a person's most psychologically sensitive pain points. Great discomfort ensues when these points are pressed or exposed, and this discomfort is usually deflected, rejected, and shielded with negativity directed toward other people or yourself or events. This is when you see the most intense vitriol come out of a person. It is not consciousness. It is the physiological poison of identity where the feeling of 'me' maintains its stronghold and is fueled by a combination of physical and psychological intensity. It is a distasteful mix of energies that cannot be dealt with directly. In the end only consciousness can dissolve, resolve, transform, and transcend this deep sense of 'I' at its core.

~ ~ ~

The Silent Self

Conscious Transformation

If your mind wanders away,
don't follow it.

Hui-Hai

THE HIDDEN meaning of all creation is transformation. Everything we can see internally and externally can be transformed into higher and higher forms of itself until it reaches the source from which it sprang, at which point it realizes itself as the source. This is not a philosophical idea. It is reality. It is truth. What makes our manifestation as human beings so remarkable is that the human form is a special kind of conduit for quickening this transformation and making it fully conscious.

Can transformation be thought of as real knowing?

It is not the knowledge, the teaching, the explaining, the understanding. It is about pure being knowing itself as the source of consciousness. This source transforms everything back into itself.

Why does the ego dislike other people?

Because by invalidating others it validates itself. The ego likes and dislikes, approves and disapproves, admires and judges based on its idea of itself, and on its idea of other people *in relation to* its idea of itself—and all of this is influenced by body type, chief feature, and center of gravity. Everyone is subject to these influences which makes for a bizarre masquerade that is the story of humanity. It is primarily a story of egos—of ghosts.

Will it help if I renounce the vanities of my life?

Renouncing external things does not lead anywhere. Real renouncement is internal. It means consciousness renouncing the illusion of 'I'.

Can you say more about how chief feature is entwined around the instinctive center?

The instinctive center and chief feature are directly linked. They are like physiological siblings which together spawn a psychological environment in which the ego can grow. One forms the basis of the body. The other forms the basis of the mind. And from both springs our sense of 'I'. You could also say that our feeling of 'I' is rooted in both. But this is just a short summary in words. It requires considerable self-observation coupled with self-remembering to understand all of this fully. It is a real question, though. A strong question. I hope you will hold onto it and investigate it for yourself.

Can we see when pure consciousness manifests itself?

Pure consciousness does not manifest directly in the dimensions of the mind and body. It manifests *through* them. The mind and body can at best reflect the influences of consciousness that echo through them. Your question shows how the mind keeps trying to grasp, pin down, and conclude the nature of consciousness, but it can never do that. Only consciousness can know itself. Somehow you have to come to this realization. It has to dawn on you like the sun dawning on the horizon of your mind.

Does the instinctive center drive chief feature?

In a sense, yes. All the other centers depend on the instinctive center for energy and health. They are all infused with this energy. And this same energy transports the influences of chief feature throughout the mind and body. So you can say that the instinctive center is a carrier of chief feature.

Does it also drive the ego?

The instinctive center and chief feature form the basis of the ego. Together they can spot the weaknesses in other instinctive centers and prey upon those weaknesses by belittling, taking advantage of, and manipulating other egos. The instinctive center can even see chief feature in another person without knowing what it is seeing. Sometimes it can see right through to chief feature at its core in another person, which disarms the other person. They feel exposed and vulnerable, and they unwittingly yield and submit. And none of it has anything to do with consciousness.

When I was asking about consciousness manifesting itself, I meant in the sense of seeing that we are aware...

What we call awareness can be conscious of seeing things, *and* be conscious of being conscious of seeing things, *and* be conscious of the fact that it is conscious of being conscious. There is also a place—what Huang Po called "the place of precious things"—beyond all of these dimensions which sees each of them.

When you speak like that the jungle of my thoughts gets more wild and confused.

Thoughts seem real but they are not. They are mental vapor. This is true not only of thoughts but of all our feelings and conclusions and points of view. They are all nothing in comparison to consciousness and the pure being at the source of consciousness. They are just noise generated by the four centers. At any time we can drop them by dropping the ego that has gathered around them and be totally free, at peace. Thoughts hold us prisoner only because we want them to. You have to stop wanting them to. You have to stop believing that the jungle is you.

What do you mean by mental vapor?

Like fog. You will discover that it is possible to see through your *entire* inner world, including the ego experiencing this inner world, as though you are seeing through a mist. You see that there is nothing solid about it. From there you settle as the void of pure consciousness.

And the ego?

It is part of the vapor. Take away the word 'ego' and ask yourself, what is this psychological phenomenon? Where does it come from? How does it promulgate a sense of identity And where is consciousness in this whole picture?

If I lined up what the fourth way calls the different levels of man next to one another, what differences would I see?

These numbers are not literal. They are symbolic. They are also logarithmic in the sense that there is not just a gap but a whole dimension between each level of man. Each level represents consciousness expanding into the next higher dimension of itself, then the next and the next and the next. But to answer your question, you might not notice anything at first. If you sat in a room with all of them for an hour, however, you might notice some things. The extent to which they were quiet, for example.

How do you understand the idea that our life is a dream?

Our lives are playing themselves out in the theatre of humanity which is a dream-drama playing itself out in the theatre of the earth and solar system and galaxy. It is a dream in the sense that it is all the projection of a series of images that give rise to form, and then consciousness believes the projection. That is what identification is: belief in and attachment to the projected image of 'I'. Enlightenment refers to when consciousness realizes this.

And yet if feels convincingly like my life?

It seems like it is all about 'me', but it never is because 'me' is a projected image that disappears in the expansion of self-realized consciousness. It is hard for the mind to fathom this because the mind itself is a mechanism inside the projection of identity. The mind is not even on the inside of the dream looking out. It is just a conception device. It turns the reflections of the perceptions of consciousness into the psychological form of concepts.

And I am there behind the mind…

Yes, in the sense of you as consciousness. At the core of your being you are the silent, delicate energy of consciousness. Don't try to push everything away. Just be this silence. The more you can *be,* the more everything else will float away and the more you will float away from everything else. This emptiness is the peace that surpasses all understanding.

Is the emptiness the lake realizing itself?

When the lake realizes itself as the lake, some of the fish in the lake try to describe the experience of realizing this oneness. This is a natural distraction that prevents the further realization of being the lakebed beyond the lake. But at a certain point consciousness sees the fish talking about oneness and presuming to be the oneness, and it surpasses them, too.

What distinction do you draw between consciousness and pure being?

Pure being is the source of consciousness, the silent backdrop of consciousness from which awareness emerges. The deepest meaning of 'know thyself' is for this bedrock to consciously recognize, realize, and affirm itself—not as an entity or identity, but as the unmanifest source of being. This is why I referred to it as the lakebed. All thoughts and emotions and sensations are the fish in the lake. Awareness is the lake they swim in. Pure being is the lakebed without which the lake could not be. Most of the time we are preoccupied with the fish, unaware of the lake, and oblivious to the lakebed.

What is the unmanifest source?

The entire visible, tangible, audible world of plants, animals, people, planets, and the universe are manifestations of form that originate in and are projected by the silent, unmanifested, invisible, intangible reality behind them. We don't usually think about this. Instead we see the multivarious forms of life in the universe and try to probe them without considering their origin and source.

How can we move closer to the unmanifest?

By becoming more and more interested in what is perceiving all this; not about what is seen and not about 'I' as the seer, but about the seeing itself and the source of seeing; that which makes awareness possible in the first place. What is that? Do you know it in the deepest part of your being? What might it be like to live from there?

Like a drop realizing itself as the ocean?

The miracle of consciousness is that each drop has the capacity to expand as and be the entire universe of consciousness because although it appears to the mind as a drop, it is in truth all one, fully united and a complete whole that is immediately connected *right now*. This is the idea behind non-localized space in physics where everything is everywhere at once, where no point is localized somewhere in space because there is no space and no time, and that everything is the same yet unique manifestation of the same unmanifest source. There is a saying that its veil—meaning how the unity of everything disguises itself—is its oneness. It is always right here in front of us. The whole thing. This sounds like superficial spiritual talk until it becomes reality for the consciousness in you.

Can you say more about how the mind reflects consciousness?

The mind—which applies to all four centers—is like a mirror or an echo chamber. It reflects and echoes not consciousness but the perceptions of consciousness. These reflections appear in different forms as sensations, thoughts, emotions, urges of ego, and more. Consciousness surrounds all of them as they reflect and echo as 'I', 'I', 'I'.

Which is what you mean by the mind as a structure...

Yes, and an empty structure. What occupies it are reflections and images that arise as reactions in response to perceptions of awareness. These reflections and images are nothing more than mental projections that are cast into the cavity of the mind the way a light is cast into the night sky. But they are not tangible. Science, for example, has never found a thought or feeling or an entity called 'I' associated with them. Nor can science measure the diameter of the mind which is both smaller and larger than science can know.

Do you believe in out-of-body experiences?

It depends. Out-of-*body* experiences cannot have meaning in the long run if they are not accompanied by out-of-*mind* experiences and out-of-*ego* experiences. To be fully meaningful, consciousness has to get outside *everything*.

Are mind and ego essentially the same thing?

When we are identified, yes. Thoughts arise as reflected images inside the mind. When consciousness identifies with these images it *becomes* the ego. When it does not identify with these images, it realizes itself beyond the mind that is reflecting them. This can also happen in reverse when consciousness suddenly realizes itself and sees thoughts as nothing more than images within the structure of the mind.

If more people become more conscious, can we end the turmoil on earth?

Within organic life on earth, and possibly within the entire universe, only humans appear to be in turmoil. Why? Because of the ego as an artificial sense of 'I'. Take 'I' away and see what happens. Imagine humanity without it. At the same time, it is interesting to consider that the ego is part of the psychological design of this human form, and that mankind is meant to live in turmoil and to suffer. According to the fourth way, this can serve two distinct purposes: one mechanical and one conscious. It is easy to suppose that it would be nice to get rid of the suffering on earth, but that is a shortsighted view.

Do good deeds make a difference?

Many people have been taught and cling to the delusion that they will be rewarded at death for having lived their life as a good person, which means different things in different cultures. But this is just a mental concept which the ego indulges in for comfort. It does not mean, however, that you should freely indulge in bad deeds. It means that the notion of 'me' as a good or bad person is just a notion that has nothing to do with consciousness or the transformation of consciousness. In esoteric Christianity, good refers to conscious awareness and evil refers to identification.

So it is really about being more and more focused in the present...

More and more focused *as* presence. You will eventually see that there is no present, just as there is no past and future. There is just the presence of awareness. All the rest is static film in the mind, including the images you see in front of you right now which you call the present. This film is not real in the sense that it is only a projection. It appears real because of the light of awareness shining through it. That is the mystery. At the core of your being you are this intangible energy of light which also constitutes the source that generates this light. But we don't see this because we are identified with the film and its constant array of images both inside us and outside us.

Are we as the person to any degree real?

Ultimately, no. Only consciousness is real. Everything else is temporal form that will evaporate sooner than you think. Even the genuine feeling of 'I' speaking as an ambassador for consciousness is not the real thing. It is, at best, a reflection of consciousness. What is casting the reflection cannot be seen or heard or touched, which is why it goes unnoticed by most people most of the time.

Can you say more about the source of awareness?

The most astonishing thing about our existence is that we can be aware of it, yet this goes unnoticed. Isn't that odd? We can be aware of everything inside the psychological world and outside in the physical universe and yet all the things we can be aware of are not aware of themselves. The only question then becomes, what is this which can be aware of everything else, and what does it mean for it to be conscious of itself? How is that possible? What makes it possible? Is there something else behind and beyond this capacity to be aware? How might that source be investigated and realized? The only way to do that is with conscious awareness. It all begins and ends with this capacity we call awareness which has the potential to go deeper and deeper and deeper into itself *as itself.*

~ ~ ~

To be clearly in original spirit
is the sole meaning of your existence.

old man Tcheng

The Silent Self

Monterey, California

2023

The Silent Self

www.ingramcontent.com/pod-product-compliance
Lightning Source LLC
Chambersburg PA
CBHW021102080526
44587CB00010B/349